Praise for Viral Jesus:

"Noah has become one of my
passionate about is loving God
make you better at both of thos
able to put it down."

- Cole LaBrant, Youtuber & Best Selling Author

"In a world that is addicted to being known, Noah initiates a very
necessary conversation of what really matters, and what actually
lasts. This is a very honest and insightful look into the way Jesus
has called us to live, not to build our own temporary kingdom, but
to build His."

- Tiffany Hammer, Elevation Worship Leader & Songwriter

It is so easy for us to get caught up in trying to find our identity in
likes and followers. In "Viral Jesus", Noah Herrin makes the
beautiful connection of how Jesus lived His life in the spotlight and
how we can follow his example in an Instagram driven world. For as
long as I've known Noah, I've appreciated how everything he does
on social media is authentic to who he is in private. I am so excited
for people everywhere to get their hands on "Viral Jesus" and feel
empowered to use their influence to share the love of Jesus.

- Chris Durso, Pastor of Saints Church, Author of "The Heist" and "Misfit"

1

"Noah Herrin is not only an incredible leader and pastor, but his ability as a writer is equally compelling. In a digital age Noah skillfully and passionately points us back to what or rather who matters most! Viral Jesus is a MUST READ!"

- Gerald Fadayomi, Speaker & Founder of the For God So Loved Tour

"I love the way Noah tackles some of the most critical roadblocks this next generation is encountering. This book is relevant, relatable, sincerely funny, and greatly helpful for those looking to live a set apart life for Christ."

- Grant Skeldon, Executive Director of Initiative Network & Author of The Passion Generation

"Noah shows us through personal reflection and practical wisdom how to refocus and realign ourselves with Jesus and his mission. I highly recommend this book to anyone who has any social media app on their phone."

- Tyshone Roland, Youth Pastor Free Chapel

"This book will inspire and challenge the reader to broaden their understanding of virality - especially when it applies to faith. Bringing Christ back to an ever changing culture is the center of this book and Noah relays the message with great truth! A must read!"

- Grayson Bearden, Pastor & Influencer

Viral Jesus
Copyright 2020 Noah Herrin
To request permissions, contact the publisher at:
NoahHerrinTalks@gmail.com
ISBN: 9798677873478
First paperback edition September 2020

Edited by Erin Taliaferro
Design by: Zach Camp

NoahHerrin.org

For my wife Maddy.

Thank you for living out the message of this book in a way that made it so easy to write about. You look more like Jesus than any person I have ever known.

To you the reader,

First of all - thank you. I'm beyond humbled you'd pick my book up.

This book is a guide to HELP you go Viral in the Kingdom of God. My prayer is that it truly is helpful, and ultimately, makes the name of Jesus great. He deserves all of the glory.

If it is helpful to you in any way - I have a favor to ask. Will you help share it? As you'll soon find out in this book, a KEY part of going viral is the "share". If this book helps, would you consider sharing it with a friend, co-worker, teammate, classmate or family member?

Finally, if you'd like to go deeper into the teachings and thoughts of this book, I've created a resource for you called the "Going Viral" masterclass. This resource is not going to teach you how to become famous online...but it WILL help with things like studying the Bible, your quiet time and reaching the lost for Jesus. It's available on my website: NoahHerrin.org

Thank you for reading my words. I'm rooting for you.

-    Noah Herrin

Viral Jesus

I'll never forget the first time it happened to me.

It was something I had been expecting, and yet, it caught me totally off guard. I had planned for this to happen. I had hoped this would happen. Shoot...I had even dreamed that this would happen.

I had felt this rush before, though at first it wasn't me experiencing it. I was just sitting in the car when my friend took the hit. That's all I needed to be hooked. It didn't even have to happen to me and I could still experience the rush... that's how addicting this was.

But when I was the one experiencing it - that hit different.

"Dude. Check your twitter."

"What?"

"You're not going to believe this bro. Get on Instagram too. NOW."
I'll never forget the first time it happened to me.

It was something I had been expecting, and yet, it caught me totally
off guard. I had planned for this to happen. I had hoped this would
happen. Shoot...I had even dreamed that this would happen.

I had felt this rush before, though at first it wasn't me experiencing
it. I was just sitting in the car when my friend took the hit. That's all I
needed to be hooked. It didn't even have to happen to me and I
could still experience the rush... that's how addicting this was.

But when I was the one experiencing it - that hit different.

"Dude. Check your twitter."

"What?"

"You're not going to believe this bro. Get on Instagram too. NOW."

I opened up my twitter account. That's when I experienced my first
hit. I had gained thousands of followers in less than an hour. I had
so many notifications that I couldn't refresh my account fast enough
to keep up. My mentions were coming in from all over the world. I
literally thought my iPhone was going to break.

I closed the twitter app and opened up my Instagram. Another hit.

My follower count had jumped from around 8,000 to almost 15,000. Hearts were dancing all over my page. People, who just minutes before didn't even know I existed, were now reading everything I had ever posted. My DM's became flooded. Friends were texting me screenshots of their friend's friends who were sharing my post.

I felt seen. I felt heard. I felt hooked.

That night I became addicted to a very real drug.
That drug is called:

Going viral.

What is going viral anyway? Maybe you live under a rock or perhaps your parents decided to shield you from the technological world. Instead of giving you an iPhone for your 14th birthday they gave you a telescope or a flute. If that's the case, I am so sorry. But shout out to all of my flute players, you're killing it.

The Webster's dictionary definition of going Viral:
A person or piece of content that is circulated or shared widely on the internet. Something that reaches an exponential amount of people or has exponential impact.

Most people don't join social media with the sole intent being to go viral however; some join social media with the simple intention of connectivity. It's fun, lighthearted and rarely time consuming. That is, at first.

It only takes a small amount of time for them to experience a social media "high". A post gets more interaction than their others, they see a viral piece of content that they relate to or maybe someone just comments something super nice and suddenly they feel like a pocketful of sunshine.

After receiving the dopamine hits that come from being seen and liked online, many of those same people who joined for connectivity are now staying for much more. They look at other online content creators who get thousands, tens of thousands or even millions of "likes" on their photos or videos and they want to experience that same thing; they want to chase that high.

Not only does going viral FEEL good...it improves your quality of life. At least we think.
In the year 2020, companies around the world have shifted their entire marketing campaigns. Instead of paying tens of thousands of dollars on ad videos, these companies are reaching out to content creators with large platforms to pay them directly for an advertisement on their video or piece of content.

Being a social media "influencer" has become a quite viable career option. In fact, today, it is just as common for a kid under the age of 12 to say they want to be a YouTuber when they grow up as it is for them to say a doctor or baseball player.

Going viral feels good. It makes you popular. It makes you rich. It makes you known. So much so, that it causes us to change our goals in order to pursue it.

That's where my story comes in.

Social media is kind of my thing. I'm in my mid twenties. I haven't grown up with a cell phone in my hand since birth but I'm not asking anyone what "viral" means either. I'd like to think I'm cool (my wife is going to snort when she reads that line).

I remember when I logged on to social media for the first time.

At 12 years old my parents let me get a Myspace. There's a good chance you might not even know what that is, so for all you Gen-Zers, it was like a Facebook page except you could customize everything about your profile page from top to bottom.

Pretty incredible right?

I had a 1969 corvette background, a profile picture that wasn't even me (it was a picture of a professional baseball player I found on google images) and when you landed on my page the beginning of a Blink 182 song began to play. I was much cooler online than I was in person and that's a scary thought.

I was thriving.

A passion for social media began to rise inside of 12 year old me. By the time I got to college I decided I wanted to study it.

I loved making youtube videos. I loved taking photos of my friends and I on top of mountain tops (making us look way more adventurous than we actually were). I loved tweeting live during football games from my couch. I loved how I was seemingly seconds away from saying something or posting something that could potentially impact thousands of people.

And I LOVED seeing my likes and my followers go *up*.

What started out as a creative outlet for me, quickly became about "growing" my platform online. I even started to get paid by brands and companies for the content that I posted. Which, as a broke college student, allowed me to pay for my steady diet of *Chick-Fil-A* sandwiches. I became addicted to the thrill of growing my online brand.

And the fastest way to do that was, of course: *going viral*.

Many times, all it takes is one time going viral. One video, photo or piece of content getting the right amount of shares and likes could change a person's life forever. If a post breaks through once, it could often lead to massive amounts of new followers and a permanent place in the social media hierarchy. One piece of viral content increases the chances of future success dramatically.

Going viral made you last. At least, I thought it did.

I started to study people who were building their online following. I wanted to know how they broke through from "every day social media posters" to the famous influencers that they now were.

I learned quickly that social media is not discriminatory. The people going viral never look the same. You have black people, white people and every color in-between. There are young and there are old. A 9-year-old can go viral playing with Play-Doh and a 90-year-old can go viral talking about world events from the couch with her husband.

Anybody, anywhere, at any time could go viral. As long as they do one thing: beat the algorithm.

A social media algorithm is a system. It's a set of rules that filters posts in a user's feed based off of the post's potential relevance to other users. Think of it like a filter put in place that attempts to figure out if content is good or not. The algorithm tries to distinguish good content from bad content by measuring engagement through watch time, likes and several other factors. The better the content scores on this unwritten social media "test" - the more people will see the content. If the content does extremely well....it might just go viral.

Sure the pretty girl who posts tons of content of only her face has a higher chance of beating the algorithm due to the amount of clueless single boys lining up in her DM's thinking they can be her "Mr. Right".

Sure Justin Bieber's video of his dog might go viral because he's Justin Bieber and people like dogs.

But going viral...is something anybody can do.

There are literally thousands and thousands of people who go viral every single day. Not because they are the best looking, not because they are already famous, not even because they paid a social media platform to boost their post to more people. They go viral because they figured out (knowingly or unknowingly) how to get their content to pass the filter put in place by social media companies. They learned to beat the algorithm.

That last line is going to be important in where we are going. I'll write it again. They go viral because they figured out (knowingly or unknowingly) how to beat the unwritten set of rules called the algorithm.

They go viral because they beat the rules.

On January 22nd of 2020, I sat in a coffee shop across from one of my mentors. It was cold outside. I remember it was so cold that I ordered a hot coffee instead of a cold one (iced coffee fam where you at!?).

We spent the first few minutes of our conversation catching up on the highlights of the month. We shared goals, wins and even reflected on some losses. Every time I met with this man we would spend the first few minutes catching up and then progress to my little black notebook that I would have sitting on the black mahogany coffee table. Inside that little black book I would have 4-5 questions jotted down to ask my mentor about. The questions could be related to anything. Marriage, pastoral leadership, friendships, sermon writing - even social media.

On January 22nd, however, I only had one thing written down in my notebook.

"Why?"

Not too long before our coffee meeting, a well known leader, entrepreneur and family man in our area had called it quits on life. It was devastating. This was a man with all of the accolades you could imagine. He was popular, he had money, he had a beautiful family - by all accounts, he was extremely successful by the world's standards.

He was even viral online. But further than that: his LIFE was viral.

But it still didn't last. He walked away from it all.

"Why?"

It didn't make sense to me. My mind kept racing back to the perfect picture his life had been just weeks before. He had what I was chasing. His instagram feed aesthetic was 10/10 online and his life seemed to be also.

He had what I wanted. How could it not be enough?

I opened up to my mentor about what was bothering me. I told him I couldn't stop thinking about the man and couldn't wrap my head around what had happened. How could someone be that known, that successful and that viral and it still not be enough.

My mentor took a long, deep breath and looked out the window. He told me he was heartbroken too.

Then He said words that I will never forget.

"What good is going viral if your life doesn't last?"

That line hit me like a ton of bricks.

If I was honest with myself - I had been trying to go viral. Online and offline, I desired more. I wanted more success, more followers, more money, more popularity, more people to look at my life and say "that's #goals".

But this path...this quest to going viral...would it really last?

How could I really *last*?

The algorithm of life and the algorithm of social media really aren't all that different. The blueprints are strikingly similar.

The harder you work, the more money you make, the more popular you are, the more power you have and the greater you make your name...the more viral you go. These standards of success become our goals, and our goals, often influence the life we end up living.

This formula for going viral has been the same for the last 2000 years.

Think of the biggest names in today's society. Names like: Lebron James, Oprah Winfrey, Justin Bieber and Carrie Underwood. They have figured out how to beat this algorithm. Their methods of getting to the top may be slightly different, but for the most part, they followed this set of rules and did so better than the other people around them, and now they have what others do not: they are seen, they are known, and their names are going to last.

At least, this is what we are told.

But what if we are wrong? What if the algorithm the world tells us we should follow is just a big lie?

Take for example Caesar, for example: the ruler of ancient Rome some 2000 years ago. He was the definition of a big-timer. They named a salad after him for crying out loud (a good one too)! He's the definition of going viral in life. He had power. His face was on money. That's how you KNOW you've made it. That honor is reserved for presidents and the monopoly man, all of which are legends.

Caesar's influence was so strong because he beat the algorithm. And yet, Caesar was constantly striving for more power, more land, and more authority. It was never enough. He murdered thousands. He plundered homes of thousands more.

How could someone *so* viral be *so*...unfulfilled? So unsatisfied?

I started thinking about other people just like Caesar. Powerful people. Successful people. Viral people. They all had two things in common:

1.) They went viral
2.) They were mostly forgotten.

16

Think about it. At BEST, their lives have become a sentence in a history book. At worst, they were left out of the history book all together and we've forgotten their name and what they accomplished completely.
They beat the algorithm but death beat them.

But there is one man whose name has lasted much longer than the monopoly man's, any president's or even Caesar's.

This man did not seem to have a shot at going viral. He was born to a poor family, He had no military background, He spent his first 30 years in a small fishing village using hand tools to build kitchen tables and Lazy Boy sofas. He did not hold any political office. He did not pursue power or fame. In fact, this man did not try to become more: He spent His life trying to become less.

This man's name was Jesus and He lived by a different set of rules. His standard was...upside down. In fact - His goals were so drastically different that people often thought He was crazy.

He openly challenged the algorithm that others were chasing after. Many times, He did the complete opposite of what someone trying to go viral would do. And yet, He became the most viral person our world has ever seen.

Caesar went for it. Jesus did too. Just in a different way.

One became a page in a history book and a $2 salad you add on to your entree.

The other...He's still going viral.

Today, people are walking the streets talking about their savior. Not the man who once owned 75 percent of the rotating world. They aren't talking about the guy who ran for president, or the guy whose face was on money, or the guy whose kingdom they said would last forever. But when you walk the streets of India; when you go to Africa, Queens, Toronto, Great Britain, Iceland, Los Angeles or wherever else you want to travel and you say the name "Jesus", people still recognize His name as the King of Kings and the Lord of Lords more than 2,000 years later. Not because He grew wealth, status or political power, but because he laid down his life for the world.

Jesus didn't go viral by going first - He did it by going last.

He didn't go viral by becoming more - He did it by becoming less.

He didn't go viral by trying to be seen - He did it through significance.

He didn't go viral by having millions of followers - He had 12.

Jesus didn't go viral by beating the algorithm - He did it by beating death.

He beat death so you could go viral, too. Not viral the way the world thinks about going viral — but a kind of viral that means so much more. He beat death so that you could go viral in the Kingdom of God. He beat death so that you could have life.

The first time I went viral I felt the rush of thousands of people crowding into my follower count on instagram. Now that I'm going viral a different way, the Jesus way, I get to feel the rush of thousands of people crowding into heaven. It's no longer about how "liked" I am. It's about how loved I am. The rush of my kingdom being built simply cannot compare to the fulfillment that comes from HIS Kingdom being built.

You can't take your following with you when you die. You can't take your success with you when you die. You can't take your kingdom with you when you die. So what good is going viral if your life doesn't last?

You can be famous on Earth but unknown in Heaven. Jesus wants you to be famous in Heaven so you can be effective on Earth.

Viral Jesus
@ViralJesus

You can be famous on Earth but unknown in Heaven. Jesus wants you to be famous in Heaven so you can be effective on Earth.

What if I told you there was a different way for you to live your life? What if I told you there was a Kingdom you could build that goes with you when you die?
What if I told you that you were actually **created** to go viral?
What if I told you there was a way that you could go viral and last?

You were destined for more than the world's idea of greatness. But in order to see it happen, you have to change what you're chasing. You might have to change your goals. You might have to change your habits and you might even have to change your definition of going viral.

The algorithm of life is fool's gold: though you might spend your whole life searching for it, it doesn't work and it definitely doesn't last.

The way Jesus lived is different. If you choose to follow this way, your life will find more meaning and more purpose than you possibly could have imagined.

You were meant for something more than a follower count. You were meant to follow.

It's time to go viral.

_____

If you want to go viral the way Jesus intends you to as His follower, you'll have to do so intentionally. You won't stumble into a relationship, purpose, and calling as good as Jesus wants you to without making it your desire and intention. We're talking about living in the kingdom of God on earth...You can't go viral by accident.

What you need is a game-plan.

This book is your game-plan. It's organized into the same 3-step process that going viral online requires. The Plan. The Post. The Share. As you read this book, you'll learn that while the process is the exact same, the method to a life that goes viral and actually lasts looks drastically different.

Here's where we are going:

1.) The Plan.

This section is the foundation to our following the ways of Jesus. These are the things that we absolutely must get right or we stand no chance of making it...let alone going viral. "The Plan" is pivotal. It consists of our convictions, our theology, and our relationship with a real and living God. Allow your heart to receive this plan and you'll be ready for what's ahead.

2.) The Post.

This section is about when reality interferes with our plan. How do we stick to the game plan when distractions and temptations are coming at us from all directions? What does following Jesus actually look like on a day-to-day basis? "The Post" is dedicated to taking action outside of your comfortable places and into the unknown: this section is where we learn to follow Jesus through the hardest parts of life.

3.) The Share.

It's impossible to go viral if your life isn't shared. "The Share" shows you how to make an impact much larger than you could possibly imagine. This section builds on your plan and your post and gives a blueprint for sharing what's taken place inside of you with the world. The share is the part of the book dedicated to crowding Heaven.

You have the game plan. Let's go viral.

The Plan

the iphone chapter

The plan.

This section is our foundation to following the ways of Jesus.
These are the things that we absolutely must get right or we
stand no chance of making it...let alone going viral. "The Plan" is
pivotal. It consists of our convictions, our theology, and our
relationship with a real and living God. The plan is what happens
behind the scenes that sets our hearts up for going viral in the
Kingdom of God.

I'll be fully transparent with you up front. It was risky putting this chapter first. There's a chance you could read this chapter and close this book forever. But there's also a chance, this chapter could change your life. I'll take my chances.

Just wait. You'll see.

GET OFF YOUR PHONE.

That's it. That's the tweet. That's the chapter.

I know I sound like your parents right now. I know you are probably picturing me as the old geezer at the table who hates fun and there may not be anything I can do now to change that. If you didn't think I was cool before this chapter (LOL) you definitely don't now.

Oh well. I'll say it again.

GET OFF YOUR PHONE.

Hear me out. I wouldn't say this if I didn't believe with my entire heart:

There may not be a greater threat to your faith than your phone.

I love what my phone can do. I have all the social media apps that you do. When the new iPhone comes out, I'll probably pre-order it even though last year's version still works fine. I'm literally writing a book based off of something you can do on your phone for crying out loud! I understand that a lot of my life is on my phone, but I also know that my phone does not give me life.

Ironically, the thing with the greatest chance of keeping you from going viral is probably your phone. We say that we have phones so we can use them. But what if they are using us?

There was a time not long ago where I stopped hearing God. I felt like my prayers came back with "could not deliver" messages. I was struggling with anxious thoughts and fears. Things that I used to have extreme clarity and vision for I began to feel completely lost about.

Then something happened: my phone broke.

I was in Israel on a trip and my international phone plan started wigging out on me. My data completely shut down. I had no access to social media, no access to my emails and the text messages from all my friends (my wife and my mom probably) couldn't come through. Is this what prison felt like? Is this what having T-Mobile felt like?

This mishap with my cell service provider only lasted for about 30 hours. I'm embarrassed to admit it but those 30 hours felt like 30 days. I caught myself opening up my social media apps mindlessly all the time only to realize there was nothing for me to refresh. I was on the other side of the world to experience the country of Israel and my phone had such a hold on me that even with it not working it was getting a ton of my attention.

By the end of the 30 hours I realized I had a serious problem. If you had asked me a few days earlier my honest thoughts about my phone usage I would have told you something like:

"I use it for work and a little bit for social media but not too much at all."

But after those 30 hours, I knew my phone had been using me so much that I had been lying to make myself feel better. That's a scary thought.

Maybe you're thinking: "So what, Noah? What's the big deal if you spend several hours a day on your phone? It's 2020 get with the times. bro."
And to that I respond: what you allow in your life unchecked usually becomes uncontrollable.

I allowed myself to use my phone however I wanted, and it led to hours and hours of mindless scrolling on apps that distracted me from real life and tangible relationships.

Viral Jesus
@ViralJesus

What's the point of keeping up with everyone else's life if it keeps you from living your own?

What's the point of keeping up with everyone else's life if it distracts us from living ours?

The craziest part is - I could spend hours online and completely forget about 99% of the content I consumed that day. According to a study done by ABC News at the end of 2019, the average American spends over 5.5 hours a day on their phone. That number increases to over 7 hours a day for people under the age of 30.

In Matthew 6:21 Jesus said "Where your treasure is, your heart will be also."

I don't have much treasure when it comes to "bling" or things that go "Cha-Ching", but what I do value a lot is my time. Time is valuable. We have a limited amount of it and none of us really know how close we are to running out of it. So time is worth a LOT.

I started doing some simple math regarding my time (simple math is the only kind of math I can do - ask my high school statistics teacher). If the average person sleeps for 8 hours that leaves us with 16 hours left in our day. 16 hours in which we have consciousness and can make decisions on what to do. Let's set aside some nice, round numbers for everyday tasks that we all *have* to do: eat meals (this includes coffee you hipsters), use the bathroom and commute to and from work or school = 3 hours. Work/school /make that cash money = 6 hours on average a day (8 hours divided by 7 days a week).
Now. If we just stopped right here - this would leave us with 7 hours left exactly to do with as we please on a daily basis. Which just so happens to be the exact average number of hours that most people under the age of 30 are using to spend on their phone. It's important to look at this with the numbers in mind, because we need to realize just how intentional we have to be with our time. Don't worry, I have a plan for that, too in the next couple of pages.

We are not living; we are scrolling, and that scrolling will quickly become our shackles, if it hasn't already.

Show me where your time is spent, and I'll show you where your treasure is. My fear is that we are storing up a treasure that is *fool's gold*. Pulling out or phone has become routine: easy and entertaining. But in exchange for this entertainment, we have lost relationships, being present to the moment, and most importantly, communicating with Jesus. If you want to go viral like Jesus, your treasure has to be the same as His: the presence of God.

Think about your first few moments waking up and the last moments before you go to sleep. Most of us start our day by depositing to an account that has the worst return on investment possible. Before we've even spoken to God we let the world speak to us about comparison, anxiety, and our individual brand. Before bed, it is so easy to pull out social media and sedate ourselves with much of the same. Instead of being with those we love, or talking to the One who loves us, we chose to spend the first and last few moments of our day with those who don't even know us.

I stopped hearing God just before I left for my trip to Israel. I thought God had gone silent on me but now I know that something else was happening.

Digital distraction leads to spiritual disconnection.

When you are distracted, you stop hearing God. You stop seeing God. You stop feeling God altogether sometimes. Where has God gone?

Maybe God hasn't gone anywhere. Maybe we just have so many apps open that we don't see His notifications when they come through.
So I'll say it again:

PUT DOWN YOUR PHONE.

Are you stressed? Are you tired? Has it been a long time since you've had a fresh moment in the sweet presence of Jesus? Maybe it's time to disconnect digitally so you can reconnect spiritually. Maybe the best thing that could happen to your relationship with Jesus is for your phone to break for a day or two. The good news is this: God wants to connect with you. He's here right now with you. He is closer than you could possibly imagine; you just have to be willing to put everything else on "do not disturb" for a little while. So maybe you're still not buying it. You think I'm the captain of the no fun club. Maybe you stopped reading this chapter and texted a picture of my book to your friends and told them to avoid it like the DMV.

That's ok. I'm going to pray for you.

Lol just kidding. Kind of.

Instead, I'm going to make you a deal: for the next few pages I am going to outline a social experiment, or rather, a phone experiment for you to try out. You could call it a *plan*. If you do these things and they do not help your spiritual life in a radical way; I vow to get on social media and tell the whole world to avoid my book like it's the DMV. In fact, I will go to the DMV for you from now on so you don't have to.

But you have to try it.

You have to follow these rules for at least a week's time. These are steps that I started to take when I returned from Israel and they refreshed my relationship with God in a way that I had no idea I needed. I believe they'll do the same for you.

Rule 1: Talk to God first.

Do not, I repeat do not, pick up your phone until you've picked up your Bible. I literally mean do not touch it. If you have to go to Walmart and buy one of those old school alarm clocks so that you don't have to use your phone as one then DO IT. Let your phone charge in a completely different room at night.

When you wake up, choose to let God's voice be the first voice you have spoken over your day. Spend time with Him before you do anything else.

I know lots of people do their time with the Lord differently, and that's awesome and jazzy and fun, but there is something about winning the morning. When you let God get your attention first, you win the morning - which leads to you winning the day.

Instead of all the potential stress that comes with opening up your phone and seeing a text that causes anxiety, or a social media post that causes bitterness, or an email from a store that you give all your money too...you get to experience the peace, joy, and hope that can only come from God. It's a game changer.

Rule 2: Be more famous with your friends than your followers.

How many times have you hung out with people and it just ended up being a group phone checking session? I can't be the only person under 30 who thinks that is the lamest thing. Why did we even get together? You could have done this exact thing from your couch or even your toilet! This isn't it, fam.

Make it a rule that when you are with friends your phone is not with you.

Remember that game "the floor is lava"? If you aren't familiar with it, basically someone says "the floor is lava" randomly and you avoid touching the floor at all costs. You jump on top of the nearest couch or trash can or dirty clothes basket. It's amazing, and the inventor of that game should win something very nice.

When you're with friends, avoid your phone like it's lava. Don't check it. No scrolling allowed. Don't the relationships with your friends mean a lot more than the ones with complete strangers? Then invest in them! That looks like being present for the good and bad times. That looks like giving undivided attention, whether you are having a deep conversation about life or doing belly flops into your neighbor's pool at 2 o'clock in the morning.

I have a hard time believing that if Jesus was on earth today in human form that he would stop the good times with His disciples to catch up on watching instagram stories...Not happening. He'd be in the moment. He'd be doing life with people.

He'd be belly flopping.

Rule 3: Cut your screen time in half this week.

This might hurt. If you're like me, this will hurt. Open up your screen time app and take a quick peek at how much time you spent on your phone last week.

Got your number?

It's probably more than you realized. I'm not trying to guilt trip you or make you cry into your Starbucks flat white. But you can't change what you won't confront. A huge step in good change is recognizing the problem.

No matter what your amount of time was for last week, I challenge you to cut that number in half. If it was 8 hours, this week get it to 4. If it was 4 then let's get it to 2.

Even if you follow rule 1 and 2, and you've got a bunch of free time leftover on your hands, find something else to do with it besides being on your phone. Meet up with a friend over coffee. Take your dog for a walk in the park. Start learning that new skill you've always wanted to try. Start chasing that dream you've always said you "didn't have time for".

Not only will this lead you to a week full of life giving things, but it will also show you that you aren't missing out on as much as you thought you were by being offline. In fact, you probably will feel just as connected with everyone online as you did before...only it took half the amount of time.

Follow this plan. I know rules sound lame. Trust me, I was the kid who tried to break all of them as fast as possible. Don't think of these things as rules, think of them as liberators. Sometimes a few rules leads to a whole lot more freedom in the long run. If you give these 3 a shot, I guarantee you your life will change dramatically. Make them a habit, and you'll never want to go back to the way it was before.

Before you know it, you're going to accomplish more dreams, have better friendships and hear from God in ways you never have before. All because you TURNED OFF THE PHONE.

the love chapter

Instagram is drastically changing the standards of what you look for in a relationship. There, I said it. Fellas: do you think she's "the one" or does she just look really good in a bikini on your news feed? Ladies: do you really think he's going to push you towards Jesus or are his 6-pack abs distracting you from who he really is (I went there)?

Once again, social media is dictating your life. In this case, it's altering your perception of what you want in a relationship! What you once prioritized in a spouse, be it wisdom or grace or patience, has now turned into what you can tangibly see on a social media feed; beautiful eyes, big biceps, six pack abs or a perfect family photo.

The goals you set for your life often end up determining the life you live. This is true of your love life as well. That's why it's so important to have a plan when it comes to your relationships. Show me your relationship goals and I'll show you how healthy your love life will look in 5 years.

If you're reading this and you've decided you want to be single, this chapter probably isn't for you. But if you're reading this and you're single and desiring a Godly plan for your love life, stick around. If you're married and desiring the same thing, you can stay too.

You *love* love. You do.

I can see it all over your face. Stop thinking about the person you love. Look, now you can't.

There are two types of people when it comes to love.

Type 1:

You're a sucker for a good engagement post on social media. It makes your heart happy when you see an elderly couple holding hands at the park. You regularly ask couples how they met and say "AWWW". You might be happily married but you still force your husband to watch chick flicks with you because you love watching well paid actors fall madly in love in 2 hours or less. On Valentine's day you buy the candy, the bear, AND the flowers. You know all the good pick up lines and you are not afraid to use them. You love, love.

Type 2:

You love, love too. You just try to hide it. You say that "you're the only snack in the kitchen", but you secretly hope you'll find love one day. When people talk about online dating apps like Bumble or Tinder you claim that the only "Tinder" you need is a 4-count Chicken Tender from Chick-Fil-A. You try to keep your emotions close to the vest, but your face blushes a little bit when you think about that special someone who probably has no idea that you think of them as a special someone.

We love, love. We were created to receive love and give love by a God who created love. It's a part of who we were designed to be.

Love is awesome...until it's not.

In today's culture, love (or the misidentification of love) is one of the biggest threats to you going viral. I've seen countless followers of the way of Jesus thrown off course by a simple relationship.

Paul actually says it's easier to just be single!

1 Corinthians 7:8-9 I do, though, tell the unmarried and widows that singleness might well be the best thing for them, as it has been for me. But if they can't manage their desires and emotions, they should by all means go ahead and get married.

Some of you just got so pumped. You just got broken up with and you're going to look that verse up and post it as your instagram caption for that fire selfie you took this morning. I can feel it.

Paul says it's easier to serve the Lord single. You have less on your mind.

Paul isn't against love. He goes on to say that if you "can't manage your desires and emotions" then it's better for you to just get married. Basically, if you can't keep it together, if you're a sucker for rom-coms or the girl across the street, just go put a ring on it.

Now, I know there is a chance somebody reading this is single with the intent of staying that way forever. If that's you, I genuinely applaud you and this chapter of the book you can probably skip. But for most people reading this book, you are like me. You fall into the category of people who cannot control their desires or emotions. You are looking for Mr. or Mrs. RIGHT. You are looking for that person you can take home to yo momma. You are looking for love.

If we truly want to go viral the way Jesus intended us to, our relationship status can't keep us from Jesus - it should actually cause us to run towards Him. That *plan* begins in your singleness.

Have you ever witnessed a relationship bloom right before your eyes? This relationship was so natural and beautiful that it almost felt too good to be true?

I was a part of one of these relationships before. Are you surprised? I've seen the movie Hitch like 11 times. In high school, I wore polo t-shirts and pooka shell necklaces. I was THRIVING.

One Thursday morning in the 10th grade I was sitting in American History Class focused, like the good student I was, on Mr. Chambers as he taught us about the Civil War (more likely I was doodling on my notebook paper and thinking about playing *Xbox* later that night, but I'm going to give myself the benefit of the doubt here in case my future kids ever read this book. That way, I can tell them to pay attention in school). So there I was, sitting there learning about Abraham Lincoln, when the door to the classroom opened wide to reveal Mrs. right.

At that moment, I had never experienced butteries in my stomach like that before (I would on a completely different level later when I met Maddy Herrin. Thanks Jesus.). A spotlight was shining on this girl as she stood in the doorway. Her face began to glow. Birds started chirping and choirs started singing and I...was *definitely* still focused on learning about the civil war(stay in school, kids!).

She walked in the door and handed a piece of paper to my History Teacher that explained she was transferring into our class from that day forward. Mr. Chambers looked around the room for an empty desk. Our class was already extremely big, so there was only one empty desk in the entire room. It just so happened that that desk was directly next to mine (It was one of those moments where I looked up at God and was like: "MY GUY". I knew God was a good God but I did not know He was a good wingman).

That semester was amazing. We might have been in history class but it was obvious (to me at least) that this girl and I had some serious chemistry. We would talk before and after class, sometimes I'd offer her a piece of gum and she even knew my name. This was going in the right direction for sure. A few months later, she stopped me outside before class and asked if we could talk at the *Dairy Queen* across the street from our school that afternoon.

I knew I had game, but I didn't know I had GAME. Are you kidding me!? This girl, asking ME on the first date? I should write a book.

That afternoon we slid into a dairy queen both where I knew she would soon be professing her love to me. What a picture-perfect-moment: both of us holding *Reese's Peanut Butter Cup Blizzards* in our hands as the sweet aroma of love and peanut butter rose all around us. This was how it was meant to be. This was spiritual.

"Noah, I have something I've been wanting to tell you." she said.

Oh, I know, girl.

"I've been wanting to talk to you about this for a really long time, I've just been nervous".

I have that effect on people. It's the necklace I'm wearing and my good looks.

"I have a HUGE crush...."

Let's get married.

"On your best friend Dillon".

Delete me.

That day I learned our love had been a lie. In fact, it had never been love in the first place. From the moment I met that girl in history class to the moment she broke my heart, I had been seeing what I wanted to see in our relationship. She obviously wasn't crushing on me as hard as I was on her.

I think the biggest problem we face in living out a Godly design for our singleness is not a compatibility problem, it's not a communication problem...it's not even a love problem. The biggest problem we face is a vision problem. We lack the vision to see things in our relationships the way God sees them.

If we saw our singleness the way God sees it, we wouldn't look at it like a sickness to be healed from; we'd look at it as a season to draw close to Jesus. If we saw our singleness the way God sees it, we wouldn't look at it as a "waiting season"; we'd look at it as a "THRIVING" season. If we saw our singleness the way God sees it, we wouldn't lack happiness because our happiness is not found in a relationship status on this earth, but our relationship status with Jesus Christ.

But do we see things like that?

Although it was never meant to be, singleness often feels like a storm. Maybe our biggest storm. We find ourselves constantly searching for the one, consumed with worry as we try and figure out where they are hiding. Before we know it, we start worrying about things we can't control and timing that's not up to us. We think more about our singleness than we do our Savior. We are so focused on *finding* "the one" that we completely miss out on becoming "the one." We long to find our person, and we long to find them fast. It can dominate our thought life. It's like there's this internal urgency that starts hitting us when we reach a certain age:

"Uh oh...I'm still single?

"Am I going to be a cat lady? Are my cats going to be my roommates forever?"

"It's fine. I'll just marry the Wendy's 4 for 4."

Instead of praying, we take the much less-effective route of worrying. We worry in our mind and call it prayer instead.

Here's the thing:

When the search for our spouse becomes more important than the pursuit of our Savior there's a huge problem. We'll never be the man or the woman our spouse needs us to be when we're trying to make things happen in the season that God is trying to mold us in. Want to know where revival in our country is? I believe we'd see the most incredible revival we've ever seen if single people simply chased Jesus as hard as they do a romantic relationship.

A God who created love and we think He's gonna leave us out of it?

In Mark 4:35 the disciples are fighting a massive storm in their boat. They start panicking so they run to find Jesus. They find him....knocked out COLD. He's snoozing on a pillow at the corner of the boat. The disciples decide to wake him up.

Jesus wakes up with an extremely curious attitude. He seems...confused? It's almost like Jesus believes it would have been more normal for the disciples to fall asleep next to him in the boat. It's almost like Jesus was hoping they would have grabbed their pillow, tossed it on the ground and started talking to him about the storm instead of trying to fight it on their own.

How long have you been fighting singleness like it's a storm instead of resting next to your savior in the boat? How long have you been searching for a relationship when you are in the same boat as the one who has the power to give you the desires of your heart in HIS perfect timing?

What if there's a different way to handle singleness? A way that sets your relationship up to last. Instead of panicking to God like the disciples did with Jesus on the boat, try praying this:

God if you say I need to be single for a while, I'm ok with that. God as long as I'm with you then I'm OK. I'm GREAT. I know on the other side I'm going to be closer to you, more like you and better fitted for a relationship anyways.

Stop playing tug-o-war with God over your singleness. Take the rope, tie it around the cross, and say, "your will be done".

Somebody pass me a pillow please. I'm trusting Jesus with this.

In John chapter 4, we read about a woman that Jesus encounters at a water well. She is there to draw water and quench her thirst. But Jesus knows this woman's story. She has had five husbands already, and now she is living with a man who is not her husband at all. She has tried to fill her "thirst" — her void — with a new man.

Jesus tells her that He is there to quench her thirst with a water that she doesn't know about. That the fulfillment and joy he gives is unlike anything she's encountered in her five husbands before.

When we allow our EYES to be the biggest decision-maker in our relationships, we don't even realize it, but we have become just like the woman at the well. We are looking for sources of water that will never quench our thirst. We may find ourselves satisfied for a moment, but we will find ourselves thirsty again, and soon. There's a difference between lust and love — between your eyes and your heart.

Lust says: what can you do for me?
Love says: what can I do for you?

Lust says: satisfy me.
Love says: how can I serve you?

Lust says: I want you.
Love says: I want what's best for you.

1 Corinthians 13:4 says that love is patient. When you fall in lust with someone, one of the first things you sacrifice is patience. Your standards start to get fuzzy as your feelings start to run rampant. You begin to feel pressure to do things you would have never thought about doing before (physically and emotionally).

If this is the case: RUN. Lust will surely mess up God's plan for your relationships.

A man of God will never ask you to be a woman of compromise.
A woman of God will never ask you to be a man of compromise.

If they try to rush you just remember: love is patient. lust rushes. Love fights for your heart. Lust breaks it.

Don't fall in lust with someone — fall in love.

But how?

Until I got married, I always hated grocery shopping. I would spend way too much time, money, and energy in those grocery stores.

The first problem I had while grocery shopping is that I would often go right after working out. I would be HUNGRY. Going grocery shopping on an empty stomach is a horrible idea. I start throwing everything that looks good to me in that moment into my cart. Instead of one box of cereal I walk out with four. Instead of a kale salad, I walk out with a kale salad, an entire rotisserie chicken, a family sized bag of *Peanut M&Ms* and a gallon of lemonade.

The second problem I had while grocery shopping was that I never made a list. I would walk into the store winging the whole thing. I didn't have meals planned out; I didn't have a list of things I needed or wanted. Whatever looked good or sounded good in the moment, I just went for that.

My wife saved me when it comes to groceries (and a lot of other things). She showed me that shopping AFTER you've eaten is actually a lot more effective. You don't buy out of impulse, but rather, because it's what you actually need.

She taught me that making a list of things that you want and need is an absolute game changer. It saves you time, money, and energy wandering around trying to do it all on the fly.

I think there's a lot of wisdom to be learned from grocery shopping. But not just when it comes to food or money.

If you're single right now: how are you "shopping" for a relationship?

Are you shopping on an empty stomach? Many single people have not made the decision to run to Jesus for fulfillment. They haven't put the season in God's hands. Because of this, they are starving for affirmation. When Jesus is your prize you are already affirmed and you operate FROM a place of acceptance and not for it.

If you're single and you're lacking that affirmation, chances are, you'll leave the "grocery store" (college, a dating site, the mall etc.) with someone who simply filled your void with affirmation. You might even call it love for awhile. But at the end of the day, hearts will break.
Because you were hungry and lovely, and confused affirmation with love.

We have to stop shopping while we're hungry. We have to stop looking for relationships until we are first content with Jesus. It's the only way we can be sure we are seeing things with clarity while dating, when standards and boundaries can become so fuzzy with emotion.

Viral Jesus
@ViralJesus

Stop confusing affirmation and attention for love.

My wife Maddy dated other guys before she met me (none of them compared to me obviously). She was in a long term relationship that ended abruptly about 2 years before I walked into her life. She struggled at first with the break up. Who wouldn't? When you spend tons of time with a person only for it to take a turn for the worst...it can be a huge blow.

For a few months she experienced all types of emotions. Some days she was fine and other days she was not. Some days she just wanted to be single and other days she just wanted to find a replacement. She ended up going 2 years being single in her mid twenties. It wasn't because she didn't have chances. My wife is drop dead gorgeous. Like the kind of gorgeous that makes people stare gorgeous. Not just that, but she's fun, creative, smart, a go getter and so much more. She's the ultimate catch. Tons of guys were interested in her. Tons of great guys tried to get her attention and couldn't.

During those two years of singleness, she became SO content in her relationship with Jesus that she wasn't hungry for anything else.

When you truly hunger for Jesus you lose your appetite for things that aren't a part of his plan.

She actually said to her mom one day: "Mom, I genuinely think I could be just as happy if I was single the rest of my life as I would be married."

What!? Who says that? In our world? Was she from another planet?

I remember our first date so well. It was a good date, but it wasn't anything CRAZY. I remember sitting across from her and realizing that I was talking to a girl whose happiness would never come from me. I was listening to someone talk who knew who she was, what she wanted and where she was going. Me? The only way I was going to be a part of that is if I could keep up. No..if I wanted any part of this girl I'd have to go to Jesus to find her. That's where she was hidden. That's who filled her up.

My "love" story (or most of the time, lack of love story) is pretty similar to my wife's.

I dated a girl in college for a long time and it didn't end up working out. I was heartbroken. I thought there was no way I could ever meet someone I cared about as much as that girl. Boy was I mistaken.

If you're reading this and you've recently found yourself in a similar situation of pain and hurt let me stop right now and encourage you in this: if you loved them THAT much, imagine how much your love for someone else pales in comparison to God's love for you. Instead of focusing on that "someone" or "that next someone" focus on having faith that God is writing your story.

I look back regularly on my life and thank God for keeping me from what I thought I wanted. His plan is better. You can take that to the bank.

When my college girlfriend and I broke it off, I felt like I had hit rock bottom. Years invested into the same person only for it to all far apart. I was distraught. I was constantly listening to LANY, Chris Brown, Rascal Flatts and just about any other artist who had written songs about break ups. I was at a low point.

A few months into the break up I hit a turning point. I remember being tired of feeling sorry for myself, and suddenly wanting to make the most of my singleness. I wanted to LIVE again. I knew I couldn't fully move on from what had been until I started looking forward to what was to come.

That night I took out a small notebook that I kept next to my bedside and I wrote "HER" at the top of the page. I began to write down the things I hoped my future wife would have. When I was done writing I began to pray over those things.

I specifically told God:

"Lord. These are the desires of my heart. If any of these desires are not your PLAN, I pray that you would redirect me. I pray that you would give my heart discernment when I meet people. I pray that you would allow my eyes to see girls the way you see them. I don't want to look for a relationship, I want to look for you. I pray that in the process of looking for you - you'll bring this girl I'm praying for along my path. In Jesus name, amen."

I must have prayed hundreds of variations of that prayer before I met Maddy.

Since our wedding, I've talked to tons of young single people who have asked the question "How did you know she was the one? Did you FEEL it? Could you FEEL it?"

Of course I felt it. But if you're out there waiting to just "feel it" chances are you are going to jump into a relationship with the wrong person. A lot of things can make you "feel it". I didn't just want to feel it; I wanted to SEE it.

See what? The things I had been praying for.
How can you expect your relationship to have standards if you never set them for yourself? If you're waiting for that "feeling", you're probably going to find it on your social media timeline — in that bikini picture or looking at that six pack. But it won't come from a place found in the 1 Corinthians 13 model. It will come from your eyes, and not from the plan that god has laid on your heart.

Pray about what you want. Talk to God about it. Make a list of the things you want in your future spouse. When they walk into your life, you'll be able to SEE it before anyone else does.
"Oh yeah, that's what I prayed for."

If you've gotten this far in the "love chapter" congratulations. I'm gonna wrap it up here. I haven't been married that long so I'm not going to pretend to know what I'm talking about when it comes to that. Instead I'll just stick to giving advice for those of you who are single. I made it through that time relatively well-off. Hopefully thirty years from now my wife will tell me I'm so good at marriage that I should write a new book on that (ha!).

Relationships are tricky. They have the potential to be a catalyst in your quest to follow Jesus and the potential to do the opposite. Don't let the world, culture, or social media fool you when it comes to relationships. They are messy. You don't wake up every day with your breath smelling like a *Tic-Tac* on the set of *The Notebook*. It's not always what social media says it is, but it can be what God intended it to be.

Real relationship "goals" are two imperfect people joined together by a perfect God: Serving each other, encouraging each other, having grace for each other when you mess up, helping each other get up, running after Jesus together. Goals aren't in the photos - they're in the process. They're found in Jesus first.

Go find Jesus, first.

the taste of grace

About a month before our wedding day, I sat my then fiancé down for a very serious conversation. I don't remember the exact words I used, but I basically told her that I knew how hard it was going to be for her to resist me once we got married. I said that it was absolutely critical that she practice self-control when it came to having babies, and that we needed to wait at least three years. Because I knew the combination of my slightly-above-average looks and my dashing dad jokes would make this request a hard one to fulfill, I promised her my daily prayers.

Almost three months later, I sat my wife Maddy back down for another serious conversation. This time to tell her I had a bad case of what the kids call: "baby fever".

We solved this problem, at least momentarily, with the adoption of a miniature golden doodle puppy named Mogley. Classic newlywed move.

Mogley is the best puppy. I know everyone thinks their dog is the cutest dog in the world, but everyone is wrong. Mogley is so cute that he makes cute dogs look not cute. Mogley is the puppy you told your puppy not to worry about.

But it's not just Mogley's looks that make him the best dog ever. He is great on the leash. He can sit, shake, and even roll over if you promise him enough treats. He even lets us know when he has to use the bathroom. He's just an awesome dog.

He's even helped me spiritually.

In the winter time, there were several times when he would wake me up in the wee hours of the morning to use the bathroom. I would stand outside freezing in my pajamas quoting scripture:

"Love is patient. Love is kind....you're about to make me lose my mind, up in here, up in here. Hurry up it's cold!". (Ok I might've added to that verse).

My wife is in love with Mogley too. She thinks he is the perfect dog... with the exception of one Saturday afternoon.

Before you can accurately picture the scene I am going to attempt to describe to you, you have to understand two things. First, you must know that Maddy is literally the real life *Sweet Home Alabama*. She's actually from the state of Alabama. She's small and blonde and she has that thick country accent that feels like it should come with a side of grandma's sweet tea. She is literally Reese Witherspoon reincarnated. Second, you have to understand that Maddy does not do germs. In fact, we are actively seeking counsel on what we should do when we have kids because BOTH of us are absolutely horrified by the thought of changing diapers. For real...please pray for us.

So, I had just gotten home from running a few errands around town. I decided to quickly hop in the shower so that I could get ready for our date night later that evening.
It started softly at first. Almost calmly. The sound of Maddy's sweet southern accent coming from our living room over the noise of the running shower.

"No. No. No. No, Mogley."

But then it went from zero to one hundred... Real quick.
"No. NO. MOGLEY. NO MOGLEY!" she yelled.

This is how I knew that whatever Mogley had just done was serious. The bathroom door swung open and Maddy said:

"Come get your son!"

Just a few minutes before he was our son. But now he was solely *my* son.

When I walked around the corner into our living room I saw Maddy, one hand over her nose and one hand with a paper towel full of the present Mogley had left us in the corner of the house. If that alone had been the problem, it would have been quite normal. After all, he was just a puppy. But as I approached Maddy I began to realize that this "present" had been much bigger than I anticipated, and somehow made its way to Maddy's favorite new sweatpants.

An absolute tragedy....that I laughed out loud at.

To this day, no matter how good Mogley is we bring up that Saturday afternoon.

"Mogley, you're such a good boy. You just better not do you-know-what again, OK?"

"Mogley, you are so obedient! You just better not do you-know-what on **DAD** OK?"

It was the one mistake Mogley might not ever be able to live down.

We all have that one mistake we can't seem to forget. For me I have several. Moments much more serious than Mogley's accident in the house.

The moments I wish I could forget are mostly tied to sin. I have moments where I've made huge mistakes hurting myself in the process and sometimes even others.
It seems like no matter how hard I try to move past them, they are always there. Sometimes I think I'm over it. Sometimes I can even go weeks or months without thinking about them, and then out of nowhere I am smacked in the face with the brutal reminders of my past.

How can we shake off our past when it so often feels like our shadow?
Where we struggle, though — God shines.

Did you know that when we accept Jesus into our hearts that the Bible actually says that God doesn't just **forgive** our sins but he actually **forgets** our sins?

Hebrews 10:17 says, " I will remember their sins no more".

Honestly, this is hard to wrap my head around. It's much easier for me to believe that God would be willing to forgive me for the little mistakes. You know, like the little white lies or the spanish tests I used to cheat on in the 6th grade. But what about the sins and mistakes that sometimes keep me up at night?

"I will remember their sins no more"

He forgets them. He throws them as far as the east is from the west.

So why do we keep remembering things that God has chosen to forget? Why do we keep trying to pay for something that Jesus already paid for? Somehow the enemy has convinced us that salvation is a goal and not a gift; that if we would just do enough good things, we will erase the past that we are trying so desperately to forget.

It's almost like we see our lives on one big scale. We feel like we must balance out our sins with good deeds in order to live a "good life".

On one side of the scale, piled high, is your sin, mistakes, and regrets. That side is HEAVY. That side is piled high like a stack of pancakes, except those things don't smell or look nearly as good as pancakes. That side of the scale is overflowing with failures. Then we look at the other side of the scale where our goodness is supposed to go. You know, our good deeds, service to others, church attendance records, times we helped the little lady across the street, etc. And that side just doesn't seem quite good enough. That side of the scale feels too light.

So what do we do? We start trying to even the scale. We start trying to earn what God freely gave to us. We start filling up our schedules with "doing good things". We make it our mission to even out our sins with our own righteousness. We start trying to prove to Jesus that He made a good choice when He went to the cross with us in mind. We start living a life that's more about impressing God than enjoying God.

Have you ever tried to impress God before? Maybe instead of memorizing scripture from your usual bible you've picked up the Old King James version instead just to prove that you're "really" saved. You started saying things like "where art thou k-cups for thy coffee pot"? But really, have you ever tried to seriously impress God? I definitely have. I've filled up my entire schedule with all of the things I thought God wanted me to do. I've done things simply because I wanted to appear close to Jesus, and oftentimes, the fastest way to seem close to Jesus is just to seem perfect and do a lot of good things...right?

Does this sound familiar to you? Have you ever strove for something? Strove for Jesus? Strove for affirmation from other believers? Strove for that spot on the church worship team? Strove to be noticed? Strove to be good?

The devil LOVES striving.

If we have any desire for our lives to go viral - we have to constantly fight to kill the striving in our lives. Striving is a viral life killer.

The devil knows if he can get you to strive he can eventually get you to die. He knows that those whose hope is in the Lord will not grow weary (Isaiah 40:31) but those whose hope is in their own strength only have so much of it. He knows that when you're striving, you are actually living disconnected from the TRUE source of life: Jesus; eventually you will get so burnt out that you might just decide to quit on your own.

Viral. Life. Killer.

So yeah, the devil is "pro-strive".

Why do you think your mistakes keep you up at night? It's not God putting those thoughts there. Remember? He forgot them when you asked him to forgive you. It's the enemy who keeps reminding you of your mistakes. He wants you to believe that the only way God will accept you is if you go try and pay Jesus back for what He did for you.

Are you tired of thinking about the pain of your past mistakes? I have good news for you.

If the devil keeps bringing up your past, you should be encouraged. He's running out of new material.

You weren't saved by your striving; you were saved by a savior. You weren't saved by your character; you were saved by the cross. You weren't bought with your busyness; you were bought by the blood of Jesus!

Your past is a place of reference now. Not a place of residency.

Viral Jesus
@ViralJesus

Your past is a place of reference now.
Not a place of residency.

Satan will say "REMEMBER YOUR SIN" but Jesus says "REMEMBER THE CROSS".

Satan will say "REMEMBER WHEN" but Jesus says "REMEMBER ME".

When Jesus Christ hung on that old rugged cross He bore the weight of every single sin and mistake that you and I have ever and will ever have. Three days later when Jesus walked out of the grave, death was defeated once and for all. Jesus was who He said He was: our redeemer, our advocate and our savior.

So if you feel like you've been living your life on a massive scale, constantly trying to even out the sides: stop right now. Salvation is not a loan - you don't have to keep making payments. Stop trying to pay Jesus back for something that was already paid in full. Just stop. Accept the free gift. Think about what it would look like to follow Jesus not because you were trying to earn his acceptance - but because you already had it.

Many times our past plan interferes with our future plan.

"But what about the things I've done. There's so many. Shoot, I even messed up this morning! I've got to get back to work to make up for that!"

There's a huge lie going around that says if you've sinned a lot you have to fight your way back to Jesus. You don't. You just have to turn around.
Proverbs 16:24 (TPT) says this: For the lovers of God may suffer adversity
and stumble seven times, but they will continue to rise over and over again.

You don't miss out on the grace of God when you fall. You miss out when you stay down instead of getting back up and following Jesus again. Your past plan doesn't have to be your future plan, because your past plan was redeemed by a person named Jesus. His plan is right in front of you; you just have to start stepping.

Let me introduce you to Bob.

I grew up in Florida where my parents pastored an awesome church. The church was located about 30 minutes from the beach. Jesus and the ocean? That sounds like the Lord speaking to me. It was a healthy church. There were all generations and backgrounds represented and it was growing.

One Sunday Bob walked in.

Bob was a rough dude. We know there are no "rough" people in God's eyes, but most of us would have looked at Bob and understood this was a man with a past that followed him around like a shadow.

Bob had recently gotten out of prison and was living out of his 1999 Toyota Corolla. He'd been trying to find work and get his life back on track when he met my dad. My dad helped him find some work and, of course, invited him to our church.

I'll never forget the day Bob accepted Jesus into his heart. It was his first Sunday at our church and when my grandfather concluded his sermon and asked if anyone wanted to accept Jesus into their heart, Bob was the first one in the altar. It was a moving experience for me to watch as a kid.

Bob jumped all-in to the community of our church. He was on FIRE for Jesus. He joined the greeter team, which welcomed people at the front of the church building every weekend, and he signed up for one of the men's small groups. Every Sunday he would sit on the front row and worship with everything he had in him. I promise you he came down for every single altar call, too. There was one Sunday my mom preached a message *for moms* and he was so excited that he responded to the message with all the other moms. Jesus had changed his life, that much was certain.

Bob was everyone in the church's favorite person. For a short amount of time.

It was about 4 weeks after Bob gave his life to Jesus when the complaints came in. Someone called my dad and expressed to him that they didn't think the best place for Bob to serve was on the greeter team. They were worried he didn't give the best "first impression" for a church as "great" as ours. People in Bob's small group started changing groups because they were tired of Bob talking about the grace of God. He was just a little too "crazy" to handle every week. People who were once celebrating the way Bob worshipped in service were now rolling their eyes and making jokes as Bob responded to yet another altar call.

Many of the people who had issues with Bob had been in church longer than Bob had been alive. They probably had forgotten more of the word of God than Bob even knew. But Bob was the one with the fresh perspective of God's grace. Bob was the one with the passion. Bob was the one who was inviting lost people to church. Bob was the one who couldn't keep quiet about the good news of Jesus Christ.

I've been around church my whole life and, sadly, I've seen this story play out dozens if not hundreds of times. Why is it that the most passionate people in our communities of faith are often the newest believers? Shouldn't it be the opposite? Shouldn't those of us who've been following Jesus the longest have even more passion, more love and more excitement for what Jesus is doing than anyone else?

How could someone like Bob be the most passionate in a room full of a thousand people that had spent years hearing of the love and grace of God? I believe it's because he embraced his encounter with God's grace.

In Luke 23, Jesus turns to a sinner hanging on the cross beside him who was moments away from his last breath. This man's scale was surely imbalanced. His life was one littered with mistakes. This was a man who would have no opportunity to prove it to Jesus that he could get it because he was glued to a cross moments away from his own death. Yet, Jesus looks at him and promises him eternity.

Just when you think: Oh, they are too far from God. Jesus says: Oh no. They are invited too."

Sometimes, if we don't see ourselves like that thief on the cross, or even like Bob, we somehow conclude that we have more entitlement to grace and therefore its nuance fades.

Have you allowed the nuance of grace to fade? Go back to the place you discovered it for yourself. I remember the wave of emotions that came over me when I understood that I deserved hell but was going to get heaven instead. I remember how the tears began to stream down my face at the reality of what Jesus did for me. How could Jesus look at a broken sinner like me and choose to take my place? It was my first taste of grace, and it tasted sweeter than anything I had ever tasted before. I knew that my life had changed.

It was that taste that turned to passion, love, expectancy, joy, and peace. It was the taste of God's grace that changed my life immediately and eternally. I had found the greatest gift imaginable and I looked at it as such. It was that taste of god's grace that filled my heart and my soul and put a desire inside of me for everyone I knew to have the same experience with Jesus that I did.

My worry for us as followers of Jesus is that if we aren't careful we can lose the taste of grace. We can forget that moment of undeserving love and freedom and in turn, become hardened and apathetic to the ways of Jesus. We can take our eyes off of the incredible gift we've received and lose sight of how truly blessed we are.

Do you feel calloused? Do you feel tired? Have you lost your passion? Do you feel like sometimes it is easier for you to be skeptical of others than it is to be *supportive* of others? Maybe it's time for you to go back to the place where Jesus found you. Go back to where He picked you up out of your darkest time. Remember that before you could pick yourself up and take a step towards Jesus, he was running to you. He met you in that moment not to condemn you but to wrap his arms around you and say "It is finished".

Bob kept showing up to our church. He kept worshiping Jesus with the same passion, and eventually, that passion began to spread around our entire church. Fresh tastes of God's grace began to take place.

You want to know the antidote for a heart that's lost passion for Jesus? It's a simple taste of God's grace.

You want to know the cure for someone who is still wrestling with the same sins? It's a taste of God's grace.

You want to know where healing from your past comes from? Just a little taste of God's grace.

Don't forget the taste.

By the time I got to high school, I honestly didn't like church much. Everybody knew me because I was the pastor's kid, which made me feel kind of how I imagine politicians must feel - always smiling and waving, despite how I felt inside. I felt fake. Not to mention, I was always having to wear khaki pants and polos to make the older people happy. That just wasn't my vibe. How was I supposed to find a girlfriend with *that* outfit?
By the time I got to college, I had completely turned my back on the ways of Jesus. I had had enough of religion. My last year of college, however, someone sent me a youtube video in a text message. The text read this: "I know you're not into preachers, but this guy is absolutely hilarious. I think you'll like what he has to say".

I opened the video with the full intention of watching a couple of minutes and going back to my vanilla latte and research paper.

41 minutes later I was crying in my room giving my life to Christ. Yes that's right. Through a youtube video.

Why? How? What could this internet pastor possibly have said that drastically changed my life so quickly?

He spoke on grace, and that day I had my taste. He recited 2 Corinthians 5:21 "He who knew no sin, became sin, so that I might become right with God."

I couldn't wrap my mind around this grace. I was blown away by this Jesus. How could a man walk to a cross knowing that you were still going to look him straight in his bloody eyes and choose to sin regardless?

See, grace is not a moment; it's not a one time deal. It's not an insurance plan that only covers certain sin. Grace continuously looks into the darkest parts of your soul and says "I'm gonna cover that, too." Grace is God's unmerited favor and love. Grace is the thing you could never deserve and will never fully understand. To God all sin is equally evil and all sinners - equally lovable. Grace is God's answer to our mess. Grace isn't just a pardon; it's a power. Grace will save your life and it will set you free. Grace is a person and his name is JESUS.

When it seems too good to be true, that's grace. That's Jesus.

A taste of what Jesus had done for me hit me that day in my college apartment and it changed my life forever.

But what happened next caught me completely off guard:

I kept sinning. I kept messing up.

I genuinely thought something was wrong with me. Didn't christians stop sinning when they got saved? Was I even really saved? It was all so confusing to me.

I remember I would have a good week or maybe a good few days only to mess up again. I remember praying prayers to God like:

"Ok God, that's the last time I promise. Watch me. I'm done messing up now".

That never worked. I had tasted God's grace but I still didn't understand how it worked yet. I still believed that some part of it was on me. I felt like I needed to balance this scale of bad and good in my life and my will power needed to get stronger.

I was doing it all wrong.
I started studying my Bible. I started studying my Bible, desperately and what I found changed everything.

There are only two of Jesus's disciples whose locations we are aware of at the time of Jesus's crucifixion. Just two of the twelve.

The first is Peter, who reminds me a lot of myself. Peter was always a little bit of an emotional rollercoaster. We would describe him as constantly "in his feelings" if he were here today. One minute he was fishing or praying and the next minute he was literally cutting a policeman's ear off with a sword! You did not want to catch Peter on a rough night's sleep!

Peter was the guy who was always the first guy willing to try something new but he was also usually the first one to mess everything up too.

Just hours before Jesus was crucified something crazy happened. Jesus looked at Peter and told him that Peter was going to deny Him...not once, not twice but THREE different times. Peter in total Peter fashion responds like this:

"No...not me Jesus. I would never do something like that. Why would I ever deny you. TRUST me Jesus. I got your back! You're my guy! I'm your guy! I'll never deny you!"

Sure enough...the prediction Jesus gave comes true. When recognized by a bystander, Peter says repeatedly that he does not know this guy Jesus.

Then we fast forward and Jesus is hanging on the cross. Without a question this is the hardest moment of Jesus's life. He is in pain, unexplainable. He is being mocked and embarrassed. He could probably use his friend Peter's company.

But where is Peter? Nowhere to be found. He is off somewhere in a corner hiding and basking in his own shame for what he had done. Instead of getting back up when he fell he stayed down. Ironically, he chose to let his sin keep him from his savior in the very moment his savior was dying for his sin.

Peter chose shame.

There is one other disciple whose whereabouts we know of in the same moment. This disciple's name was John.

I'm not going to lie to you, I've always thought John was a little bit...dramatic. When you read his gospel (the book of John) he always refers to himself in third person by calling himself "The one who Jesus loved". Can we just agree that that feels like something someone really into themself would do? Like I am sure the other disciples were probably annoyed by John.

"Relax bro...we get it, He loves you."
Though he might've seemed a little dramatic, I came across this little detail that changed everything: John was the only disciple of Jesus who was with Jesus at the cross.

How could twelve guys (the disciples) follow Jesus and see all the incredible things they saw and only ONE of them be there with Him in his darkest moments? How could this happen? How was it that Peter could be hiding while John was laying at the foot of the cross in the same exact moment?

Maybe it was because John was on to something.

"The one who Jesus loved".

John's focus was always on those words. Maybe it's not a coincidence that the one disciple who was not focused on his love for Jesus, but Jesus's love for him, was the only one there with Him in the end. John's focus was not on proving his love for Jesus but simply reminding himself of Jesus's love for him!

When things got tough for Peter, he ran away from Jesus because of shame.
When things got tough for John, he ran to the cross because of love.

You are the one who Jesus loves.

Stop letting your failures keep you from your Father. When you let shame keep you away from Jesus, it has the opposite effect that you want. The best possible place you could go when you fail is to the cross - towards Jesus, not away.

Religion: "I messed up. Dad's gonna kill me".
GOSPEL: "I messed up. I need to call Dad."

Viral Jesus
@ViralJesus

Religion: "I messed up. Dad's gonna kill me.

Gospel: I messed up. I need to call Dad.

If you think that by following Jesus removes failure from your life — just look at Peter. He got to follow Jesus in the flesh and he failed daily. But Jesus ended ups building his CHURCH on Peter. Peter failed but was still chosen. You might have fallen but you were still chosen. You were made to live a viral life for Jesus Christ despite your failures. But you have to get back up.

Jesus uses people who mess up. He died for them anyways. He died for me anyways. He died for you anyways. Real love isn't about keeping score. It's about losing count.

As you continue down this path of going viral in the kingdom of God, you will fall. It's not how many times you fall that will determine if you make it - it's how many times you decide to get back up. You've been forgiven. Make plans NOW: when you fall, you're going to run right back to Jesus.

You're the one who Jesus loves. Go get another taste of God's grace.

something is missing

1 Peter 5:7 (NIV)
Cast all your anxiety on him because he cares for you.

Matthew 11:28-30 (MSG)
"Are you tired? Worn out? Burned out on religion? Come to me. Get away with me and you'll recover your life. I'll show you how to take a real rest. Walk with me and work with me—watch how I do it. Learn the unforced rhythms of grace. I won't lay anything heavy or ill-fitting on you. Keep company with me and you'll learn to live freely and lightly."

I wish you could've been there the day I bought my wife's engagement ring.

I had never done something like that before. I had no experience with diamonds or gold. The most expensive piece of jewelry I owned was a fake gold chain I received from one of my college roommates in exchange for my American History notes.

I guess you could say my notes were the "golden standard". Or not. That's fine too.
Walking into the jewelry store that day, I was a nervous wreck. Anger began to swell up inside of me when I realized college had not prepared me for this moment. Why was I forced to take statistics but never taught how to be an adult? I was *sure* I was about to become a statistic:one of the many guys who got his fiancé an engagement ring she secretly hated.

It was a beautiful day at the beginning of October. The weather was already starting to feel amazing in Tennessee as Fall was approaching. I had a hot vanilla latte in my right hand to help soothe my nerves as I was trying to play it cool looking at the diamonds through the glass counter.

But the lady behind the counter did something unexpected. She asked if I knew what kind of "cut" I would like.

What was this a Great Clips?

Did they cut hair at this place too? I don't know. Give me the fade. Leave the bangs a little longer than the rest. That's what my lady likes so give me that.

I think she could tell by my silence I had no idea what she was talking about.

So she responded with another question: "Do you know what kind of clarity you'd like to have?".

Clarity. Now that's a word I knew. Give me as MUCH clarity as possible. Yes. Every great relationship has clarity. I'll take some of that.

If you're reading this and you actually know something about diamonds, you might be able to appreciate how much fun the saleswoman at the jewelry store had that day. Shoot, I had fun, too. The entire process of picking out Maddy's ring and planning our engagement day was one of the best experiences of my life. I remember the feeling of uncontrollable excitement as I picked her up from her parent's house. I remember the outfit she wore. I remember the way my hands started to sweat as we walked into the restaurant. I remember trying not to cry (and failing) as I got down on one knee. I remember the feeling of shock when she actually said yes (this was truly an underdog victory for the ages).

But I also remember another feeling as we walked back to the car that night holding hands. I remember the feeling of her ring touching my finger...and realizing for the first time that I didn't have a ring on mine. Absurd.

I mean — I knew this was how it worked. I knew the girl got the ring and the guy had to wait. But why? Have you ever thought about this? It's completely unfair. It's an injustice to guys everywhere. Besides, don't the girls *want* the world to know their man is taken? Don't you want everyone to know *this* catch is off the market? We don't need anything special. That night I would've taken a ring pop to get rid of the feelings of missing out.

Since our wedding day I've lost my wedding ring several times. The same ring I was overly dramatic about not having, I actually lost the second day of our honeymoon. You read that right. I walked around Mexico for thirteen hours with my left hand glued to the inside of my pocket out of fear that Maddy would discover my naked ring hand. I have never been more anxious in my entire life.
Here's the thing about losing my wedding ring: It was embarrassing. Yes. It was hard to admit. Yes.

But it did not change the fact that we were married.

It did not change the covenant that had been made just two days earlier. It did not change the love that we had for each other. It did not change her last name back from Herrin.

Something was just missing.
Maybe you're reading this and that sentence describes exactly how YOU feel. You're in a relationship, too. A relationship even more important than marriage. You're in a relationship with your Lord and Savior. You know Jesus Christ personally. You believe He died for your sins. If you died today you'd spend eternity with Him in Heaven. None of that has changed.

But if you are honest. If you are *really* honest...you can't help but feel like something is missing. You can't help but feel like there has got to be more.

Why is it that on a daily basis you hear more from your anxiety more than you do from your God? Why is it easier for you to worry than worship? Why is it so hard for you to find joy? Why is it so hard to find rest for your soul? Why isn't God speaking to you? Why do you find yourself questioning if God even cares about the things keeping you up at night in fear? Why can't you seem to actually go viral for the Kingdom of God?

Why does it feel like something is missing?

Maybe you're like me and you've been frustrated. Maybe you've read scripture like Matthew 11:28-30 where Jesus says you can live "freely and lightly" through Him and you've thought: *either Jesus is a liar or I am NOT doing this right. I feel a lot closer to "bound and heavy" than "freely and lightly"*.

These feelings are no strangers to my life. As someone in their mid-twenties, I know what it's like to grow up facing the challenges of our generation: the rise of the digital age, the added fear of things like school shootings, social media comparison, pornography at our fingertips, constant noise, and a social landscape of acceptance that seems to change its standards by the day.

Anxiety, fear, and depression are having their way with us. We're facing it. We're dealing with it on a level unlike we've ever seen in the history of humanity. Our generation is struggling. We're looking for a way out. We're looking at the Church for the answers, and we're not finding much. Why? Because for the most part, something is missing there, too. We're having incredible services and events on Sunday's that aren't changing our Monday's. We're being inspired. We're hearing some genuinely great stuff. But something is still....

You get the point.

I reached a place in my life where I was desperate for something more. I was desperate for my anxiety to no longer have the last say over my life. I was desperate for life, and life abundantly. I was desperate for the words of Jesus to be more than just words. I wanted them to be *real*. I wanted to test them instead of tweet them. I wanted to apply them instead of acknowledging them. I didn't need any more hype; I needed help.

1 Peter 5:7 (NIV)

Cast all your anxiety on him because he cares for you.

This was always one of my favorite verses in the Bible. I got to cast my anxiety on Jesus? Incredible! I hated that stuff anyways.

The problem was that no matter how many times I told myself to cast my anxiety on Jesus, I continued to find myself holding on to it. Why couldn't I just let go? Why did anxiety repeatedly show up in my life even though my Bible told it didn't have to?

I believe it's a simple matter of trust: you will never cast until you first believe that Jesus cares.

You will never trust Jesus with your anxiety until you first know how much He cares for your soul. Do you trust Jesus? Do you *really* trust Jesus? Until you truly trust Jesus you will always have anxiety lingering around in your life. If you're reading this and you are weighed down by stress and anxiety in your life, your focus should not be on getting rid of that weight, but rather learning to trust Jesus fully so that he can take that weight from you.

A great way to tell if you truly trust Jesus is to stop right now and ask yourself this question: "What am I worried about right now?" Where you worry most shows where you trust God the least; where you worry most shows where your anxiety controls you most.

Worrying is proof that you've bet against God.

Viral Jesus
@ViralJesus

Worry is proof that you've bet against God.

Let's split 1 Peter 5:7 into two parts. Part one:

"Cast all your anxiety on HIM"

Why should I?

Part Two:

"Because He cares for you."

Why should you trust Him? Because He cares.
Why should you cast your anxiety? Because He cares.
Why should I give him my worry, fear and anxiety? Because He cares?

Maybe you are wondering: *how do I know that He truly cares though?*

If you ever want to know how much Jesus cares just look at the cross. Look at the scars on His hands and on His feet where he was nailed to a tree instead of you and me. If you ever want to know how much Jesus cares, just remember that while you were still a sinner, He died for you. He didn't wait for you to clean yourself up or get your life together, but in your lowest moment He willingly took your place. Where you deserved death He gave you life. Where He deserved life He willingly took your death.

If you ever want to know how much Jesus cared...just look at the cross. But don't just look at the cross, really think about it. Think about how long He stayed on the cross.

At any moment, Jesus, the son of God, could've called it off. He was experiencing some of the most excruciating pain imaginable while He hung in front of all of Jerusalem. It would've been totally understandable if He had decided the pain was too much to bear. In fact, with one whisper to His Father in Heaven, legions of angels would have swooped down from Heaven and taken Him back up into the Kingdom of God. Jesus had the power to end it all. Those Roman soldiers and six-inch-nails stood no match for the army of God. Jesus could have left. The pain would've been over...but His mission would have been incomplete.

It was not an army that held Jesus to the cross. It was not the nails or the swords that kept Him on that cursed tree. It was not the ropes that kept Him tied up. What kept Jesus on the cross for hours upon hours was His unexplainable. passionate, unrivaled, reckless love for you.

Does He care about your school situation? HE CARES.
Does He care about your relationship with my parents? HE CARES.
Does He care about your finances? HE CARES.
Does He care about your anxiety? HE CARES.

Does He care about you? HE CARES. And His track record of caring is unlike anything you will ever find from anybody else. You can trust Jesus today. He cares for you. Stop holding onto the worry and the anxiety and cast it where it belongs: into the capable and loving hands of Jesus.

John 14:6 (NIV)
Jesus answered, "I am the way and the truth and the life. No one comes to the Father except through me."

In this scripture from the book of John, Jesus calls Himself 3 things:

1.) The Way
2.) The Truth
3.) The Life

As followers of Jesus, the first two of these we struggle very little with. Of course we believe Jesus is the *truth*. If we didn't believe that, we couldn't call ourselves Christians at all. Of course we want the *life* that Jesus promises us. Nobody wants to be bound by sin or spend eternity in hell. No thanks; I'll take life.

It's the 3rd thing that Jesus calls Himself that is much trickier to grasp; "The Way".

Would you say that you follow the "ways" of Jesus? Would you say that you are like Him? It is very easy in the world we live in to believe Jesus is the truth, desire the life that He promises, but ignore many of the *ways* in which He lived while He was on this earth.

I don't want you to confuse what I'm saying. I am not encouraging you to go out and try to earn God's love or salvation. You never could. That's the opposite of what Jesus is saying in John 14:6. He is saying that you need Him. This verse is not an encouragement to strive in your relationship with Jesus. I am simply saying that if you believe he is the truth and you desire the life that He promises, but you ignore His ways, you will always feel like something is missing in your relationship with Jesus.

If you want to experience the full life that Jesus promises you must be willing to adopt the lifestyle that He lived. You need His "ways". This was something the early Jesus followers were really good at. In fact, the earliest version of the Church wasn't called the "Church" at all. It was called "The Way''. This early movement of Jesus followers was filled with people who were so adamant about living the "Way" Jesus did that they were referred to as it!

Tens of thousands of people flocked to join this movement in a very short amount of time. It wasn't based on cool clothes, trendy pastors, or minimalistic spaces; it was built on the lifestyle of a man that had modeled Holiness. And it was attractive. It was a new way to do life. It was a way where you could cast your burdens on the Lord. It was a way of life where one could live freely and lightly. "The Way" is still accessible for us today.

Fast forward to today, and you'll see a word that offers a completely opposite way of doing life. This "algorithm" of life that we've talked about, is easy to see in every stage of life, but especially in our schedules. When we are stressed, anxious or worried, we buy into the lie that the solution is doing more. If we'd just schedule more, work more, make more money, get more followers or have more success on this earth, maybe just maybe it would take all of the stuff weighing us down away. The problem with that plan is that it almost always does the opposite.

When we try to fight anxiety and worry by adding more things to our plate, we actually will find ourselves being distracted into a spiritual oblivion. We get so stressed, so hurried, and so focused on things that do not matter eternally that Jesus himself could be standing next to us at the grocery store checkout line and we would not even notice Him.

As followers of Jesus, we must fight this outlook at all costs. It's one big distraction and will absolutely rob us of any chance of following Jesus the way He intended us to. Our chances of going Viral in His kingdom will plummet. The busier our life gets, the easier it is for us to fall away from the ways of Jesus, and those are the ways that offer the real change that we are after.

One of the ways that Jesus lived that I find so interesting is that Jesus was never in a hurry. He lived His life at a very specific, sometimes slow, pace. And it drove His disciples MAD. They regularly found themselves frustrated at the speed of Jesus. The disciples wanted Him to move faster, heal more people, travel to the next town faster, etc. Jesus always lived in the moment. He was not concerned with being in a rush.
Jesus had a specific pace because He knew that life is not about the destination; it's about enjoying God in the process.

Recently, I was preaching at a church and a small elderly woman, who looked to be around 80-years-old, came up to me to talk. To my shock, she told me that she had been following me on Instagram. This had to be the coolest 80-year-old of all time. She had a gram!? She followed me!? 80 years old!? This is gangster stuff.

Then she asked me a question. She said:

"Noah...why do you stay so busy? Every time I get on *the Instagram* it seems like you are doing something. Your schedule is just crazy! Why??"

Her question kind of caught me off guard. I remember that I laughed a little bit and replied:

"Well...The devil doesn't take days off so neither should I, right?"

I'll remember her response forever. She shot back at me:

"Why is the devil your role model? Jesus showed us that we need to rest."

I couldn't agree with that little old lady more. In fact, we do need to add more to our lives; it's just more of the stuff that matters eternally and less of the stuff that distracts us from His kingdom. We need more of His presence, we need more time in prayer, we need more time resting and practicing Sabbath, and we definitely need more of Jesus.

We've all been given this small little time on earth. The Bible calls our time here a "vapor". In other words it will be over faster than we can blink. I don't want to spend my blink weighed down over problems that I was never meant to carry. I don't want to spend my time here focused on things that I will not get to take with me into eternity.

If you're reading this and you feel like something is missing in your walk with Jesus, stop and ask yourself: what have I focused my life on? Am I focused on making this one little second great or am I focused on a relationship with the creator of the universe with whom I'm going to spend eternity with? Maybe, just maybe, this question won't just change how we handle our problems, but it will change the way we live.

Imagine a generation of young people going Viral for Jesus. What would it look like if a group of people became so satisfied in Jesus that we stopped seeking anything else as passionately? What would it look like for a group of people to intentionally slow down to pursue the ways of Jesus over the ways of this world?

He's better than anything this world has to offer and His WAYS can be your ways. Will you slow down long enough to let it happen?

I polled high school students and college students about what some of the top things were that caused anxiety and worry in their lives. What I found was that many of the same things that cause anxiety in their lives cause anxiety in mine, too. Sure there were some exceptions — I hate wrinkles in my clothes more than most people hate anything in their entire life (I really do pray for me), but for the most part; anxiety is caused by the same things in all of our lives: finances, relationships, health, our future, school, careers, etc.

All of the things that cause anxiety have a shared trait: we can't control them.

We can try our best to control them, sure. Sometimes we can even do a really good job of controlling them. But even for those of us with the best of circumstances, we have no idea when one area of our life is going to spin out of control for whatever reason and cause anxiety to come running back into our life.

So how do we deal with anxiety then? What are our options?

Option 1:

I want you to picture yourself standing in the center of an empty Target shopping center. Your girlfriend/boyfriend has wiped the entire place out, so there is nothing in the Target but you. There you are walking through life completely unfazed by anxiety because again, everything at Target has already been bought so you can't lose any money by purchasing more things from there.

All of a sudden a massive cardboard box drops through the roof and hits you on the head. The box bounces off of you and lands beside you on the floor. This box is labeled "finances" as it represents the anxiety that has suddenly shown up in your life because of bills you can no longer afford. Or maybe an unexpected cost that you don't have money to pay for.
Then another box falls through the roof and hits you. This time it's labeled "health". A virus comes out of nowhere (COVID-19) that nobody knows how to treat. You get a bad doctor's report. Or maybe you are just really stressed and you've put on too many pounds and now you feel tired all the time. This box hits you and lays beside you as well.

A third box falls from the sky labeled "your future" and zoinks you on the arm. It represents the anxiety that you feel anytime you start thinking too much about the uncertainty of your future. Everyone else seems to have their life path figured out but you can't even figure out how to put the corner sheet on your bed still. How do people sleep at night not knowing what's coming next!?

Just then, another box comes streaming down and hits you. This one is labeled "relationships". I remember the anxiety that came from this box SO well. I was going to be single forever, I thought. I was absolutely sure that I was going to be a guy living in an apartment with 8 dogs all by myself. Just me, my dogs and Reese's Puff Cereal every night while everyone else was married with kids. It used to stress me out so much.

Then 10 other boxes fall from the Target ceiling labeled all sorts of different things that represent the anxiety that so easily interrupts life.

Picture me: surrounded up to my eyeballs with massive cardboard boxes.

This is the exact way we look when we choose to handle our anxiety by letting it interrupt our life anytime it wants. We find ourselves trapped, unable to move the way Jesus intended us to: freely and lightly. Jesus could be over on aisle six, but we cannot even see him because the anxiety is blocking our view. We think thoughts like, "Where is Jesus in all of this mess? Why has God left me alone? Why does it feel like something is missing?" And the entire time, Jesus could be right next to us. Anxiety is great at blocking your vision and causing things to look much bigger than they are.

But there is a second way to handle the anxiety.

Option 2:

2 Corinthians 10:5 "And we take every thought captive and make it obedient to Jesus"

Another way to say this (the Noah Herrin translation) "And we catch every thought and make it obedient to Jesus).

We started this chapter off by examining how you can cast your anxiety on Jesus because He cares. BUT: before you cast it, you have to catch it.

Back to Target:

The boxes start falling from the ceiling on you again, but this time you are ready to catch them. Here comes the finances. The bills, the lack of income...it's scary. But you choose to catch the box this time because you remember in Matthew chapter 6 Jesus says that the birds don't even worry about what to eat, because God takes care of them — how much more does God care for you than the birds? You're good. God's gonna provide like He always does. You catch the box, and you place it down beside you.

Here comes the box labeled "health". This time you remember that one of God's names is literally "Healer". He has a track record of beating all sorts of disease, disorders, and even death. What health problem is too great for the Great Physician? NONE. You catch the box, and you place it down behind you.

Then a box labeled "future" comes crashing down through the roof. The future is unknown and scary. But then You remember that Jesus said there was no place He wouldn't go with you. And if Jesus is in the boat with me then no storm scares you, because every storm bows at his whisper. You don't have to know the future when you know who is holding it. You catch the box, and you place it down behind you.

Here comes a box labeled "relationships". It's so hard to see past heartbreak. It's so hard to see past broken and past relationships. But then you remember that God said He'd give us the desires of our heart. And if it's a true desire for someone to be married, then He will work it out in His timing. And if you thought you loved the last person you were with, just imagine how much more you are going to love the one God is preparing for you? You catch the box, and you place it down behind me.

Box after box begins to fall through the roof. But every time, you catch the box and you place it down behind you. You don't wait for the cause of anxiety to hit you; You catch it at the door. You catch it the moment it tries to box you in.

The scene looks different now. No longer are you surrounded by boxes, but now, there is a massive pyramid of boxes behind you. You are free to move wherever you want to. If God is telling you to go left, you can go there freely. If God is telling you to go right, you can go there lightly.

Here's the craziest part: the things that cause you anxiety are not absent from your life. In fact, they are right behind you. You just have a plan for anxiety now. The anxiety is not gone, but with Jesus, its' control over you IS gone.

All of the people around you can still see the things in your life that *should* be causing you to live a stressed out and worry filled life. But instead they see something different. Those that you interact with would describe you as having a "burden that is light". They would say that you are living a life that is free and simple; one that is filled with joy.

God gets glory.

The thing the devil sent into your life to pester you with is now the thing that you get to praise Jesus for using in your life. You get to point to Jesus and say that He is better than anxiety. You get to lift your hands in worship, despite your circumstance because you've casted it all onto someone who cares. Though you will live in a stressed out world, you get to live a life that is free and light and any time someone looks at your life and wants what you have, you get to tell them about your savior: Jesus.

Something is missing. My fear, my anxiety and my worry.

Thank you, Jesus.

The Post

come through dripping

The Post.

This section is about when reality interferes with our plan. How do we stick to the game plan when distractions and temptations are coming at us from all directions? What does following Jesus actually look like on a day-to-day basis? "The Post" is dedicated to taking action outside of your comfortable places and into the unknown: this section is where we learn to follow Jesus through the hardest parts of life.

Not long ago, my wife and I took our ministry's leadership team to the beach. You read that right. If you are a part of our team we take you to the beach. I'll tell you how you can sign up later.

It was the best weekend. We had deep Jesus conversations, got a little sun tan, and of course we ate lots of Chick-Fil-A (If you know me you know that I always eat lots of Chick-Fil-A. As a matter of fact, if you're doing your Christmas shopping right now — I wear a size Chick-Fil-A gift card). I have never been to another fast food restaurant where the line is wrapped around the building three times and I still willingly pull into the drive-thru because I *know* I'll still somehow get my good in 29 seconds flat. There was one time when I went inside to order and the cashier was a guy I went to highschool with. The entire time he took my order he called me "sir"...like we didn't go to high school together. I was like "bro...blink 3 times right now if you're in danger".

They are the best.

Anyway, on the second day of our beach retreat, we loaded up into our cars and pulled into the Chick-Fil-A drive-thru line on our way to the beach. I was driving my car and had four leaders inside with me. We pulled up to the drive-thru window and what we saw shocked us all.

The young lady working the Chick-Fil-A drive thru line was....crying. Crying! This is NOT what I was expecting. Actually, this was the last thing I was expecting to see. The joy of the Lord is supposed to be their strength? What was going on here?

**Disclaimer: At this point, I am going to tell the remainder of the story from two different perspectives. The first perspective will be that of my own. The second, will come from the perspective of the leaders in my car.

From my perspective:

I looked at the girl who had tears running down her face and asked

"Is everything ok? What's going on?"
She proceeded to hand me two full bags of glorious chicken and waffle fries and told me that the car in front of us had paid for our entire meal. Over $50 worth of food! I couldn't believe our luck! I grabbed the bags of food and started checking to make sure we had everything we had ordered. Then I looked back at the girl in the drive thru and said:

"WELL PRAISE GOD. HALLELUJAH. FAVOR AIN'T FAIR. GOD IS GOOD ALL THE TIME. AND ALL THE TIME GOD IS GOOD".

Then I drove away.

From the perspective of the 4 ministry leaders in my car:

We pulled up to the Chick-Fil-A drive-thru window. Our Pastor, the coolest, best looking and funniest pastor in the world was driving. (This isn't a direct quote, but I am fairly confident this is what they were thinking. Ok. Carrying on.)

To our surprise, the lady working in the drive thru window was crying her eyes out as we drove into view. Pastor Noah asked her what was going on and she replied saying that the car in front of us had paid our entire bill. Then she handed Noah the bags of food. As Noah started looking through the bags of food, she continued speaking and said: "I've been working for the past hour and a half, and you won't believe it, but, every single car for almost 90 minutes now has paid for the car behind them. It's been the craziest and coolest thing I've ever seen. I am just getting so emotional over the goodness and generosity of people. God is so good."

Right as she finished speaking, Pastor Noah looked up from the bags of food and looked at the woman working and said:

"WELL PRAISE GOD. HALLELUJAH. FAVOR AIN'T FAIR. GOD IS GOOD ALL THE TIME. AND ALL THE TIME GOD IS GOOD".

Then he drove away.

.....
THEN HE DROVE AWAY.

I probably have never looked more like a fool than I did in that moment. Possibly hundreds of cars of generous people paying for their neighbor's meal...then the pastor shows up, grabs his meal, and says DEUCES!

Yikes.

Somehow I completely missed the second part of the woman's conversation with me in that drive thru. I was so focused on the Chick-Fil-A in front of me, that I missed the bigger picture.

How many times do we make the exact same mistake? How often do we look at the situation instead of our savior?

We try to find provision instead of going to the Provider.
We try to find the healing instead of going to the Healer.
We try to make a way instead of going to the way Maker.
We try to build a life instead of going to the One who gives it.

There's a story in Matthew chapter 14 (starting in verse 22) about a man named Peter who made this mistake. Peter is in a fishing boat with 11 of his best friends trying to sail across to a place that Jesus instructed them to go. But as they begin to make the trip, a huge storm breaks out. They begin to fight for their lives as winds and waves pick up all around them. After about seven hours of fighting this terrifying storm, they see a figure that they think is a ghost walking towards them on the water.

Peter has a lot of courage. He speaks up and asks if it's Jesus walking on the water. Then he says something really crazy:

"Lord, if it's you, have me join you on the water".

Then Jesus says something even more wild:

"Come. Join me".
This story confused me for a long time. Because of a scripture I had memorized in 2 Timothy 1:7 that says this: "For God will never give you the spirit of fear, but the Holy Spirit who gives you mighty power, love, and self-control."

If God will never give me a spirit of fear, then why was Jesus asking Peter to do something *so* scary? (Can we just stop and agree right now that what Jesus is asking is absolutely terrifying? This is scarier than your wife going to Target with the credit card on a Saturday morning in the Fall when the pumpkin decorations are out!)

This wasn't Jesus asking Peter to join him in the wave pool at *DisneyWorld*. This was in the middle of a storm that was *so* powerful that it had professional fishermen scared for their lives. And Jesus looks at Peter and says, "Come. Join me on the water".

That. Is. Scary.

That. Is. Terrifying.

That. Gives. Me. Fear.

So if God doesn't give us a spirit of fear, then why does he ask us to do things that make us fearful?

There is a huge difference between a "spirit of fear" and the feeling of fear. A spirit of fear is when you let fear win. The feeling of fear is

Viral Jesus
@ViralJesus

A spirit of fear is when you let fear win. The feeling of fear is an opportunity for your faith to win.

an opportunity for your *faith* to win.

A spirit of fear is when you let fear stick around. It's when fear comes into your life and resides in your decisions, thoughts, and plans. It's when you begin to let fear dictate your life. But the feeling of fear? This is a natural part of following Jesus. Fear is a part of the faith process.

I would argue that if you never feel fear, you probably never need faith. Do you actually need faith at all if you aren't a bit scared? Do you actually need to put your trust in a God who is bigger than us if we can handle everything all on our own? I don't think so. If you are safe; if you are in your comfort zone, you don't have to rely on faith, because you already have proof.

Let me put it this way: I have an amazing wife. She is hands down the best person I have ever seen when it comes to loving people. She makes nice people look not nice. That's how nice she is. So if she ever wanted to give me advice on loving people, it wouldn't take a whole lot of faith for me to take that advice. This isn't a scary thought to me. It does not take faith for me to trust my wife when it comes to loving people, because I have seen it multiple times before. I have proof.

But. A few nights ago my wife came to me excited about a new chicken recipe she wanted to try out in the kitchen. Now, *that* was scary. At the beginning of our marriage I'm pretty sure my wife burnt ice cream one night. She has a ton of strong suits but cooking is not one of them.

When she told me she wanted to cook chicken for me, I was already looking up the *PizzaHut* number just in case things went south. But to my surprise, about 30 minutes later, I bit into the greatest piece of chicken I have ever eaten. Yes, even better than Chick-Fil-A. I couldn't help but think how I never would've experienced that incredible piece of chicken if I had let my worry or fear of Maddy's cooking keep me from believing in her.

Fear is an opportunity for faith to rise up and *win* in your life.

The reality is that God will ask you to do scary things. He will even ask you to go to scary places. But He will never ask you to do it alone. He will never ask you to go somewhere that He is not going to go with you.

God is not using fear to test you. A good teacher would never give a test on something that they haven't already taught on. God is a good teacher. If you feel fear in your life it's not a test; it's a sign that He already trusts you enough to gather the faith to overcome that fear. You've been taught; you are prepared. You will not be alone.

In Matthew 14:22-33 Jesus asks Peter to join him on the water. He asks Peter to do something scary. But in the verses coming before that, Jesus and the disciples are sitting with thousands of other people who are hungry. The problem was that they only had a few loaves of bread and fish. Jesus does the miraculous and turns this little lunch into enough fish and bread to feed all of the thousands of people around him.

You know what that was? The teacher, teaching the lesson.

He was showing the disciples that He is not defined by my odds or statistics. He was showing Peter that when He says to do something that you can trust Him to take care of the outcome. He was teaching Peter the very thing He would need to do later that night surrounded by waves and wind: Trust Jesus.

Back to the story:As Peter looked out of the boat towards Jesus he was surrounded by water. This water represented his fear.

The Bible says that Peter got out of the boat, even though he was surrounded by his fear, and began to walk towards Jesus.

This is INCREDIBLE. He's not walking on concrete, hardwood floors or ceramic tiles...our boy Peter is moon walking on H2O!!

It's important to notice though: when Peter begins to walk on the water, the water does not disappear. It's impossible to walk on water and not get wet just like it's impossible to follow Jesus and still not be a little scared sometimes.
Sometimes following Jesus requires you to do it dripping.

How did you do it? How did you have faith in that season of your life?

I did it dripping.
How did you even sleep at night knowing your bank account was negative and more bills were on the way? Weren't you terrified? Weren't you scared of the possibilities?

Absolutely. But I kept my faith in my Jesus. I came through dripping.

How did you not fall apart when your girlfriend dumped you and you thought she was the one? Did that not wreck your hope? Did that not ruin your spirit?

I was crushed. It was hard. But I believe His plans are bigger and I came through dripping!

Fear might be close, but Jesus is closer.

Practically speaking, how do we fight fear when it shows up unexpectedly in our lives?

Matthew 14:24 says that the disciples were fighting the raging storm from their sailboat and "the wind was against them in the boat". Fast forward to verse 30 as Peter is walking on water. The Bible says "Peter looked at the wind and began to sink". Peter looked at what he was up against and began to sink. He lost sight of the big picture, and focused back on what was right in front of him.

When you focus on what is AGAINST you; you'll sink. But when you focus on *who* is *for* you; you'll rise up, and your faith will increase.

When Peter was looking at Jesus, he was walking on water! But when he looked at the wind, he immediately fell short. We do the same thing. It might not be a gust of wind that tries to sink you in this season of life (although it could be if you're reading this on a sailboat I guess). But for you what might be trying to sink you is your relationship status. It might be the uncertainty of college on the horizon. It might be your weakness. It might be finances. It might be compared to people around you.

I don't know what is fighting against you today, but I know that if you focus on it, you'll sink just like Peter.

How do you fight fear? You look at the right thing.

See, if you would focus your sights on Jesus instead of your bank account, you would remember that in Matthew 6:26, wherein Jesus said to look how the birds of the air never have to worry about what to eat and yet God takes care of them. How much more valuable are you to God than them?

If you would focus your sights on Jesus instead of listening to the label of "single" and taking it as a negative, you would remember that no boy or girl can fulfill you like Jesus, anyways. You'd remember that sometimes He gives a "no" because He has a better "yes".

If you would switch your sights on Jesus instead of your weaknesses, you would remember that in the kingdom of God, it's through your weakness that Jesus actually gets the most Glory. That through your weakness you would find strength in Jesus. You'd remember that thing that you think disqualifies you actually is what qualifies you.

If you'd focus your sights off of his/her *Instagram* profile and back to Jesus, you wouldn't feel the need to compare yourself any longer. You would remember that God said you were fearfully and wonderfully made and that there is literally no one else like you on this planet.

We have to put our eyes back where they belong. Stop looking at what is against you. Start looking at who is for you. He is stronger. He is greater. He is worthy. He is with you.
It's time to come through dripping.

Before we go, we have to talk about the end of the story. This is where it gets good.

At first, the water represented Peter's fear. But when Peter lost his focus and lost his faith, he fell into the water, and the water took on an entirely new meaning. At this point, we could say the water represents his failure.

Peter was literally drowning in his failure. Then Jesus picks Peter up and they get into the boat. This is where it gets WILD: *Matthew 14:32-33 And when they got into the boat, the wind ceased. And those in the boat worshiped him, saying, "Truly you are the Son of God."*

So let me get this straight. Peter falls into the water, which now represents his failure. He is completely soaked in his mistake. Then he gets in the boat and immediately begins to worship Jesus?

Maybe it's still not hitting you the way it did me. I read these verses and I had a thought: Was Peter even *dry* yet?

Had he even had time to dry off from his failure before he came to Jesus? Or was he still dripping wet?

Matthew 14:32-33 And when they got into the boat, the wind ceased. And those in the boat worshiped him, saying, "Truly you are the Son of God."

The moment Jesus pulls Peter out of the water, the significance of the water changes for a third and final time. It started representing fear. Then it became Peter's failure. But as Jesus pulls Peter up, the water changes to represent redemption. It signifies the grace of God dripping all over Peter's life. What a savior. That Peter could fail in front of all of his friends and the Lord of his life and yet, there Jesus was, to turn the water into something worthy again. *Ephesians 1:7 "In Him we have redemption through his blood, the forgiveness of our trespasses according to his riches and grace.*

Maybe you're reading this and you feel a little like Peter. Not the Peter who is moonwalking across the ocean, but more like the Peter drowning in his failure and mistakes. You've failed. You've fallen. You're struggling. It's affected how you worship. It's affected how you think. It's affected every part of your life. Maybe you've even thrown a few towels over yourself in hopes that nobody would notice the mess that you are. Maybe you've been focusing on the wrong thing in your life.

But today is your day. Jesus is reaching out his hand. He's here to cover your mistakes but not with a towel. He's here to cover your mistakes with His blood that he shed for you on the cross.

Peter could've ran in shame but the first thing he did when he rose up out of the water was to run and worship. He ran wet. He ran soaked. He ran dripping.

It's time to come to Jesus dripping. Dripping with fear. Dripping with failure. Dripping.

It's only in the presence of Jesus that your mess becomes a miracle.

So stop waiting. Come through dripping.

build the boat

Telling someone you love them for the first time has to be one of the most nerve-wracking experiences of all time. Especially when that person is out of your league. That was the case for my now-wife and I. Only, she was several leagues outside of mine.

But if you noticed I used the word "wife" in that sentence. Aka God is still doing miracles. Hashtag moving mountains. Hashtag praise break. Hashtag...ok I'll stop.

I wanted to tell her that I loved her for several weeks. I had even practiced saying it out loud in the car several times to get used to the feeling of it coming out of my mouth.

I was nervous. I wanted to get it right. I wanted it to be special. Then it hit me.

A few friends, Maddy (my now-wife), and I had planned a trip to Hawaii that summer. We were going to be spending a week on the beautiful coast of the island Kauai, and I could not think of a more beautiful place to tell the woman of my dreams that I was madly in love with her.

I had it all pictured in my head: I was going to surf up with coconuts in both hands. Usher was going to be there singing in the background. My hair was going to be looking on-point as I casually strolled over to where Maddy was sitting on the beach. I was going to sweep her off her feet, tell her I loved her and ride a dolphin to dinner that night, where we would eat lobster and celebrate.

She deserved that. She deserved the best.

Our second day in Hawaii I woke up to the sound of the sliding glass door at the back of our *airbnb* opening. I was sleeping on a pull out couch with one of my friends, and I looked up, to my surprise, to see Maddy quietly walking out the back door. My alarm clock read five AM. Not a time I ever want to be awake.

But, I became worried about her and jumped out of bed to see what was going on. When I got outside, I saw her standing next to the ocean looking towards the waves. Oh no, I thought. Does she sleep walk? I ran up to her and asked her what was wrong. She explained to me that she was not feeling very well and that maybe the fish she had eaten at dinner the night before had not settled well. She just needed some "fresh air" she said.

I don't mean to sound dramatic here, but it was like I heard the audible voice of the Lord say "Noah, this is your time". I grabbed her hand and we started walking down the beach.
It was truly one of the most beautiful moments of my life. Shortly after we had begun to walk down the coast, the sun began to rise to our left. Birds began to chirp. Fish began to jump out of the water, and there was not another sign of another human being in sight. Just the woman of my dreams, me, and the cast of *Finding Nemo* swimming a few dozen feet from us.
There was no surf board or Usher, but this would do just fine.

Finally we got to the end of our stretch of beach, and I stopped Maddy and turned her around to where we we're facing each other squarely looking at one another.

"Maddy...I want to tell you something" I said. It was all or nothing now.

I stared deeply into her gorgeous light blue eyes.

"I love you".

There. I said it. Relief filled my entire being.

Then she looked back at me. She stared into my dark brown, kind of average eyes and she took a deep breath and whispered:

"I think I'm going to throw up".

Then she ran to the bushes.

Yep. Welcome to my life.

I love telling that story because it's real life. And, of course, because she's now my wife, and that failure ultimately led to an altar with all of our friends and an amazing wedding cake.
Just a few months after we stood on that beach in Hawaii, we got engaged. We posted the classic photo on *Instagram* of me down on one knee, and our whole world commented to congratulate us.

On the outside, it was picture perfect.

But a quick peek beneath the surface and you would see tons of stories just like the one I told you. Stories of embarrassing failures, arguments, and even ugly moments that we aren't proud of.

I wouldn't have it any other way.

Because REAL relationships take place beneath the surface. Things that are truly worthwhile and things that have any chance of lasting have to be tested first. It's absolutely necessary to have a plan for following Jesus, but our response when things don't go to plan is just as important.

Chances are, if my relationship with my wife had been all surface-level with no trials or complications for us to work through, we'd have a picture-perfect instagram with an imperfect, fake marriage. Our marriage would likely falter at the first sign of conflict.

Most of the time it's the finished product that gets celebrated, but it's the process that causes it to happen. We love what makes it to our social media feeds but we are built by what happens behind the scenes.

My wife went to The University of Alabama. They are pretty good at football down there. Their longtime Head Coach (who might be the greatest football coach of all time) always says:

"Trust the process".

I think you should, too.

In today's Christian culture, we see the same thing. We love the viral moments of following Jesus more than we do the beneath the surface ones. Conferences, camps, revivals, leading worship, sharing at small groups, preaching, attending a bible study, meeting your favorite pastor, sharing catchy quotes on instagram....all of this is good stuff. There is nothing wrong with doing any of these things. On the contrary, they're amazing!

But these are the "viral" moments of Christianity. If these things are the foundation of our walk with Jesus then we are living out a relationship that is all post and no power; the look of a Jesus follower without the lifestyle.
We might be saying and sharing the right things, but then we would be missing out on the Kingdom of God manifesting itself in our everyday lives. And most of the time, it goes unchecked by those people around us. Why? Because their energy is going to the same place as yours: the profile and not the process. We are called to go deeper than that.

One of my favorite stories in the Bible is the story of Noah. He has a great name. The best name (besides Jesus) in my opinion, and no I am not biased.

Many times when we think of the story of Noah we think of this cute little story kids read in kid's church: God was going to flood the earth. He told Noah to build a boat and put animals inside of it, and now we all have dogs in our living rooms. Unless you have a cat, and in that case, I'll pray for you.

But if we reconsider the story of Noah as an adult, we get to see it from a whole new perspective. The reason I love the story of Noah is that it's a story in which the power comes from behind the scenes. It's a story about the process. It's a story about endurance. You probably know how the story goes: God comes to Noah and tells him to build a boat. Noah obeys and gets to work. But Noah did not become the proud owner of a new yacht the next day. In fact, most Biblical scholars believe it took somewhere in the neighborhood of 120 years for Noah to complete his task. 120 years.

Can you imagine doing anything for *that* long? Noah truly lived out what it means to be faithful

Imagine the dinner conversation the day Noah heard from the Lord:

"Hey honey...I'm going to quit my job. To build a boat in the backyard".

"Oh really???" *probably Noah's wife.*

"Yeah. Really! God told me to do it!" *probably Noah.*

"OK. Like a fishing boat?" *probably Noah's wife.*

"Think more Carnival Cruise Ship." *probably Noah.*

This had to sound absolutely *insane*. Even if Noah's wife was super supportive of this (which we have reason to believe she was, at least on some level) can you imagine what she must have felt like after 20 years of this? Surely they stopped getting invitations to the neighbor's house for tea and crumpets (I don't know why Noah just became British, but just roll with it). Everybody in Noah's neighborhood thought he was crazy. He was surely the laughing stock of the city.

30 years in. "Hey Noah! Why are you still out here in these woods??"

Because God told me to. I just gotta keep building the boat.

60 years in: "Noah! You crazy old man. You've been out here for 60 years without a single thing to show for it. Where's the flood you talked about bro??"

I just gotta keep building... the boat.

80 years. 90 years. 100 years. 110 years.

Can you imagine what would've happened if Noah had quit in year 119? What a tragedy that would have been. But he didn't. For Noah, the goal was not popularity or fame. His goal was simple: faithfulness.

I've come to realize that it's easy to be faithful at the beginning. Diets are really easy on day one. The idea of willingly eating grass and exercising every morning is something we all get excited about on day one. We have the six pack in our head and we can see our "summer bod" already coming into focus. Man, we look good. But staying faithful to a diet is much more difficult on day ten. This is why, on day ten of your diet, I see most of you in the drive thru line at Chick-Fil-A. I don't blame you. The Chicken is blessed. But your diet - not so much, apparently.

It's easy to be faithful on the honeymoon. Woo hoo! This is exciting! Marriage is awesome. My spouse has never done anything wrong! I don't even think they poop!

But what about year 10? Do we wake up just as excited about the gift of marriage then? Do we love and serve our spouse the same way after all that time has passed?

Being faithful is hard. But being faithful is worth it.

You see, God only has one measurement of success. When we get to Heaven one day, He is not going to say, "well done my good and famous servant." He won't say, "well done my good and rich servant." He won't say, "well done my good and powerful servant." He will either look at you and say nothing or He will look at you and say "well done my good and FAITHFUL servant".

Do you want to please God? Be faithful. Do you want to go viral? Make your goal faithfulness - not any of the other stuff.

Albert Einstein said something that has deeply resonated with me:

"It's not that I am the smartest. I just tend to stick with problems a little longer than most people".

The truth of this statement was expressed a different way in the Bible. Galatians 6:9 says: Let us not become weary of doing good. For at the proper time we will reap a harvest if we do not give up.

If you don't give up, you win. It's that simple. But it's not just you who wins, it's the people around you who win. Your friends win, your city wins, your community wins. The world is impressed by what you start, but it is transformed by what you finish. Noah didn't give up. He didn't let what others said around him affect what God had spoken to him. His goal was not pleasing man his goal was simply to please God...and the world was never the same because of it.

What does going viral have to do with the ark or building boats?

In the world, going viral is all about results. But in the kingdom of God, going viral is all about faithfulness. Want to do something big for God? Doing something small faithfully. Say yes to him today, then do it again tomorrow.

Viral Jesus
@ViralJesus

Want to do something BIG for God? Do something small...faithfully.

Before you can truly go viral for Jesus you have to choose ahead of time how you are going to respond when your life gets hard. If you don't choose to make faithfulness your goal in advance, you'll lose your way the moment it starts to rain. But if you choose to make faithfulness your goal, your life won't just be about Jesus Christ; it will be proof of Him.

Fast forward to the end of Noah's story; the ark gets built. The flood comes just like God said it would, and Noah is inside the massive boat with his family and his own homemade zoo. He takes a photo for *Instagram* with him and his wife on the deck of the boat sitting on top of Fred the giraffe (probably).

What a viral moment. A huge, viral moment that would have been impossible without thousands of smaller, faithful ones.

A bystander would have thought: *wow! The boat floats!* But we know that faithfulness made it float. Don't put the emphasis in your life on floating. Put it on faithfulness.

If you want your life to truly go viral, it's not about the big step of faith as much as it is the small steps of faithfulness. It's about the little things that no one else sees. It's about the mornings in the word of God. It's about the small prayers you pray that no one else knows you do. It's about the constant state of seeking God's voice and listening to Him when He speaks to you.

I have watched so many Christians fall for the trap of following the results. This shows up in many different ways. Hopping ministries, jobs, cities, callings, etc. Always looking for the new "sexy" move of God happening somewhere else. What I've learned in my time following Jesus, is that the deeply satisfying moments of following Jesus often happen when you stay. Long term impact is slow and steady, not fast and hurried.

Don't be someone who follows "the move of God". No. Be someone who follows the God of the move. Don't be someone who follows results. Results come and go. Follow Jesus, He's not going anywhere.

If you've read this chapter and you still don't know where to start, I'll leave you with this parting word of advice:

Focus on being faithful today. Repeat the process Tomorrow.

stop eating the cookies

My wife bakes me chocolate chip cookies all the time. All. The. Time. If you ever wanted to know what marriage was like, let me just tell you right now: It's awesome.

A few nights a week we unwind by watching a TV show, and eating freshly baked chocolate chip cookies. It's spiritual. We've moved past the honeymoon stage and entered the cookie stage, and it's absolutely amazing.

There are some nights she rounds the corner of our kitchen with a glass plate of cookies in her hand and the aroma of hot freshly baked deliciousness wafts throughout our apartment. It's literally such a beautiful experience that sometimes I can do nothing but stretch my hands to heaven and thank God for his marvelous blessings.

It *is* a blessing. But recently I realized that this "blessing" might just get me in trouble. You see...I have an all-in personality. If I'm doing something, I want to do it 110 percent. If I am on a run with my puppy, I want to make sure I beat him back to our mailbox. When I was in 4th grade and got into *Pokemon*, I wanted to collect them all so I could whoop every single person who stood in my path at recess. When my Nana was about to beat me in *Monopoly*, I stole a few extra dollars from the bank so that I could come out on top (not proud of that one, but I DID win).

So, a few weeks ago when my wife decided to bake 16 chocolate chip cookies one night so that we'd have some for the whole week... I ate all 16 in one night. I was all in.

In the moment it felt right. They tasted amazing. They looked amazing. They smelled amazing. BLESSINGS BLESSINGS BLESSINGS. I ate one. I praised God. I ate another. I thanked the Lord for His faithfulness. I ate a third, and I thanked Jesus for the *Pillsbury Dough Boy*. I told myself several times that night: "ahhh I'll just have ONE MORE".

Before I knew it every single cookie was gone.

The next day I was hurting badly. I learned that eating 16 cookies in one night, no matter how good they looked, was not a good idea. I learned that *more* is not always what it's talked up to be.

Maybe you're reading this and you are thinking "well, duh bro. You ate 16 cookies!! What did you think was going to happen? *More* will make you throw up!"

Maybe you don't struggle with wanting more cookies, but maybe if you were honest with yourself right now you'd say you do struggle with wanting "more" out of your social media. You want more followers, you want more likes...you want more.

More almost always seems like a great idea in the moment but indulgence can be a very dangerous thing. I titled this chapter "Stop Eating the Cookies", but what I really meant was "stop letting me think that more likes and followers is going to fix my problems; stop letting me think *more* is going to make me happier.

In the algorithm of our society, "more" is the first rule to going viral. We live in a culture that is constantly telling us to do more, to get more, to make more and to BE more. This algorithm says that the way to purpose, happiness, and fulfillment is simple: you just need a little bit more.

This algorithm is a lie and we have a choice on whether or not we listen to it. We can decide to believe the lie of more and spend our life trying to crowd people into a follower count, or, we can spend our life trying to crowd people into heaven. One will leave us with a huge stomach ache. The other, will allow us to go viral in the Kingdom of God in a way that brings so much more purpose to our life than we could possibly imagine.

You don't go viral when you become successful, or get a platform. In the Kingdom of God: you go viral when Jesus is enough for you.

Stop eating the cookies, they are making you sick.

The location of production for goods is important to manufacturers. If you don't believe me, just ask a company like *Nike* or *Apple* if it matters where their products are made. Products made in places like China or Taiwan are much cheaper than products made in America or Australia due to the kinds of materials used, cost of labor, and so much more. However, the greatest factor that determines a product's cost to produce is the number of products being made.

If a product is mass-manufactured in a country like china, its value is much less than an individually-made product in America. When there is only one version of that product, the product's value increases significantly.
I think a huge reason why we find ourselves so obsessed with wanting more online is because we value ourselves like a product being mass produced. We forget that when God created us, He did not make us in a mass production assembly line. He formed each one of us, handpicked and crafted in our mother's womb, so unique and beautiful that our value in His eyes is astronomically greater than any other thing He created.

Your Job is not what gives you value; your academics don't give you your value; your success doesn't give you your value; the size of your platform doesn't give you your value. None of those things make you more or less valuable. What determines your value is *who* made you and *where* they made you. You are a one-of-a-kind masterpiece created by the same God who created the stars you look up at in the middle of the night. The same God who created the most beautiful places on Earth created you and said that YOU were his prized possession. Just think about that! You are SO valuable.

It bums me out to know that some people look at the sunset or a shooting star and think "WOW. God is so amazing!" but then look in the mirror and think "ugh" as if He didn't create both.

There's an absolutely iconic quote from one of the greatest movies of all time (The Lion King) where Mufasa looks at Simba and says "Remember who you are". If you want to see through "the illusion of more" in your life, then you have to remember who you are. You are a child of God. You were created in *His* perfect image. You are the temple of the Holy Spirit. You were fearfully and wonderfully made. You were designed with a purpose and for a purpose. You don't need to be more, Jesus already said you are enough.

Most of the time it's the world that tells us we need to become more, but sometimes even the church jumps in on the bandwagon. Be VERY careful of any Christian, leader, or pastor who talks more about your destiny than they do your Savior. God did not create you so that you would accomplish great things. He created you first and foremost to be with you. Going viral has never been about working for Jesus. Going viral is all about being with Jesus.

Viral Jesus
@ViralJesus

Going viral has never been about working for Jesus. It's all about being with Jesus.

Social media is filled with people talking about "the process". This idea of "I haven't arrived yet but one day I will". People think that God is hiding them for their "destiny" or that their platform is going to be here before they know it. That COULD be true but chances are...it probably isn't (don't hate me). That doesn't make me a hater, that makes me real. Guess what? You can have the same joy and happiness and fulfillment and purpose without ever "making it". That's the whole point. That might be the very reason you stumbled upon this book: to stop waiting to "make it" in life (like the people you follow online) before you start enjoying the greatest relationship you have access to: the one with your heavenly Father.

For those of us who are attempting to follow Jesus and go viral for Him, your biggest temptation will probably not be money, power, or fame. Your biggest temptation will be to think more about the things we want to do for God than we actually think about God. When we put the things of God over God himself, they actually can become idols in our life. We are not the main character of the story. And thank God! What a boring and limited story that would be. But lucky for us - Jesus is the main character and he allows us to be a part of that story.

Now, before you say something like. "I just want to grow a platform so that I can be an influencer and influence people for Jesus" let's think about the word "influence".

The definition of the word influence, according to Webster is: someone's ability to have an effect on someone that produces change.

The key is that influence produces *change* in others.

Because of the definition of influence, we know that none of the following things are influence because they do not lead to change in people on their own. What influence is not:

- Networking
- Social media clout
- Platforms

Jesus, by the very definition of influence, is the greatest influence of all time. His life has led to hundreds of millions of people changing. And He's just getting started. How did He do it? He didn't even have social media or the internet at all!?

Jesus influenced people by serving others, with His prayer life, by being a good neighbor, by being in constant communication with God and by being obedient to what God spoke to him. Oh yeah, and He had 12 followers.

Your capacity to be an "influencer" has nothing to do with your social media following or platform. Your capacity to influence people has everything to do with how you follow Jesus.

Want to be an influencer? Follow the guide left behind by the greatest influencer of all time.

1.) Love God.
2.) Love Others.

_____

Philippians 4:13:
"I can do all things through Christ who strengthens me."

Pretty amazing verse right? When I read this verse I can just feel my biceps getting bigger. I feel like I can take on the world! There's nothing I don't have the strength to do, accomplish or succeed in! Right?

Philippians 4:13 is one of the most taken out of context verses in all of the Bible. Many followers of Jesus will isolate verses like this from their context and think that this verse is about doing great things, fighting battles or accomplishing the impossible. But when you read the verse in its' context you see that it means something completely different:

Philippians 4:11-12 "For I have learned to be content whatever the circumstances.I know what it is to be in need, and I know what it is to have plenty. I have learned the secret of being content in any and every situation, whether well fed or hungry, whether living in plenty or in want."

Wow.

Philippians 4:13 isn't about my destiny or the things I'm going to accomplish...it's about being content. Paul isn't writing about all of the great things that you can do - he's writing about all of the great things that have already been done FOR you. He's trying to say stop making other things your prize. Stop believing that more of what the world is trying to offer you is going to make you happy.

For so long I thought Philippians 4:13 was what David had tattooed on his chest when he killed Goliath. I thought it was a verse that Paul had written after doing amazing things for Jesus. I thought it was a lesson that you could only learn from achieving, but now I know it's a lesson you can only learn by accepting what Jesus has already done.

There is only one "more" that will satisfy your soul, and it is more of the one who created it.

You won't just wake up one day living out Philippians 4:13. You have to *choose* to be content. You have to choose to stop pursuing more of the things that do not matter in the Kingdom of God. You have to choose to stop comparing your life to everyone else's online. You have to choose joy.

Yeah Marriage is going to be awesome but so is your singleness. Yeah your dream job is going to be awesome but so can the one you have right now. Yeah your future is bright but so is your now. Don't "someday" yourself out of your own life by wishing you had someone else's. You have Jesus right now, and because of that, you have everything you need and more.

A few practical tips for social media:

1.) Use social media. Don't let it use you.

- Stop checking it all day every day. Set specific times you are going to be online. If you don't, your social media apps will tell you when to be online.

- I personally try to use it this way: (Check in the morning after quiet time, check at lunch, check at dinner). This is plenty of time to stay connected without wasting my day.

2.) The unfollow button is your friend.

- If you are following a bunch of people who cause you to stumble, unfollow them. If you're a guy trying to be pure and you're following girls who post a bunch of bikini photos — UNFOLLOW THEM! If you're a girl following a bunch of bloggers who cause you to be jealous and envious of their picture perfect life — UNFOLLOW THEM.
- James 1:14-16 talks about how sin starts with desires and desires start with thoughts. If every time you open social media the people you are following cause you to have thoughts that aren't from Jesus, do yourself a favor and hit unfollow.

3.) Stay accountable.

- Give at least one other person (who you trust) your social media passwords. This accountability helps so much. We are human beings and we are weak people when tempted - helps yourself out by giving someone else access to your DM's so you won't be tempted.

trust fall

Jesus replied: "You don't understand what I am doing now, but someday you will." John 13:7

"Do you trust me?"

This has got to be the scariest question of all time. When someone asks *this* question, it is almost always followed up with them asking you to do something absolutely bonkers.

Remember the movie Aladdin? He floats up to the top of a castle on his favorite rug from *HomeGoods*, stretches out his hand to Princess Jasmine and says "Do you trust me"? WHAT?
Then there was Nicholas Cage (who is arguably the greatest actor of all time). Remember when he was holding the Declaration of Independence in one hand as he reached out his other hand to his future blonde lover in the movie National Treasure? He stared deep into her blue eyes and said "Do you trust me"? WHAT?

On a more personal note, a lady came into my grandpa's church one time and wanted to play her tambourine during service. It was a risky decision. That had never been allowed at our church before and it could have easily been a huge distraction to the congregation. She looked at my Grandpa with a pitiful smile and said "Do you trust me?".

She then proceeded to play that Tambourine louder and with more passion than I had ever seen anyone do anything before. She went *Rambo* on that *tambo*.

When someone asks you "do you trust me" you never know the end result of that trust is going to be great or a total failure. Unless, of course, the person asking for your trust is God. Then it's a whole different story.
In the story of Daniel chapter 3 we learn about three men named Shadrach, Meshach and Abednego. For the sake of not wanting to type out all three of those names anymore than I have to, we will refer to them as "SMA". The story of SMA is wild, and if you haven't heard it, I'd highly recommend you stop right now and read it for yourself before you go any further in this book.

In short: A very powerful king creates a very grand image that he wants his people to bow down and worship to. SMA are so passionate and firm in their relationship with God that they refuse to bow. The king threatens to throw them in a fiery furnace if they won't bow (he had some anger issues for sure). SMA still refuse to bow. The king has them tied up, and thrown in the furnace like he said he was going to do. The furnace is SO hot that when the guards throw them into the pit, they are burned alive. Then, to the king's shock, he looks into the furnace and sees four, not three men, walking around completely fine in the middle of the fire. The king claims the fourth looks like the son of God. They are no longer bound, and they seem to be completely unbothered by the oven that they are currently in. The king has the men removed and begins to worship the God of SMA.

WILD, right?

The story of SMA is not a story about fire or kings or furnaces. This story is about trust. It's a story where God asked SMA a simple yet terrifying question: "Do you trust me"?

God never told SMA that they weren't going to burn. Go read the story — that part is not in there. In fact, there was no guarantee at all that SMA weren't going to become a three-piece Kentucky Fried Chicken meal. And yet...SMA trusted anyways. They trusted God without the whole picture.

This is a theme we see throughout the Bible.

In the Old Testament, the Israelites fled Egypt and headed to the Promised Land. The only problem is that God never told the Israelites *where* the Promised Land was located. He never gave them the whole picture, either. Because the destination was never the point — trusting in God was the point.

Over and over again, God proves to us that we do not have to see the end of the story to trust him in the middle of it.

Viral Jesus
@ViralJesus

You don't have to know the whole story to trust God in the middle of it.

But that doesn't always make trusting God easier though, does it? We can read story after story of people who put their trust in God and God always comes through for them. But if we are honest, we struggle believing God will come through for us. At least I do.

Why is this?

I believe it's because the devil is a master at cropping the photo. Imagine this: Your life is this beautiful, huge, HD, intricate photograph. It was created with the finest attention to detail and its price is invaluable. *But*, because you are not God, you cannot see the whole thing. In fact, you can only see a small portion of it. The part you can see is small, but it's plenty to tell that this photo is beautiful and worth it and exciting. There is so much reason for joy.

But here comes the devil and he is so good at cropping the photo even smaller. He crops out all the reasons for joy and hope and peace and excitement and he only leaves the areas of uncertainty and anxiety and fear. His greatest aspiration is to try and get you to focus on the cropped version of your life so that you will miss out on the full photo that God sees up in heaven.

He speaks to you with words like: "How can you focus on the good when you don't have the full picture? How can you have faith when you don't know what tomorrow is going to bring? How can you know the picture is actually beautiful when this season is so ugly?" But while the devil is a master at cropping the photo, we serve a God who is a master artist.

You don't have to see the whole picture when you know a God who does. You don't have to have it all figured out when the Creator of the universe is your friend. Don't let the devil crop out the beauty that God has created in your life. In fact, sometimes the most beautiful parts of the photo are the ones that you didn't know were there, but trusted in a God who did.

I love the story of SMA so much because they did not know what was about to happen, but they trusted God anyways. Notice what they said to the king right before they were thrown into the furnace; "King Nebuchadnezzar, we do not need to defend ourselves before you in this matter. If we are thrown into the blazing furnace, the God we serve is able to deliver us from it, and he will deliver us[c] from Your Majesty's hand. But even if he does not, we want you to know, Your Majesty, that we will not serve your gods or worship the image of gold you have set up."(Daniel 3:16-18)

They did not try to convince the king that they were right. They didn't feel the need to post all of the reasonings behind their decision on social media. They did not feel the need to respond to their haters or the people who disagreed with what they were doing. They literally looked at the king and said "we do not need to defend ourselves in this matter".

You do not need to defend obedience to Jesus. You will not have to explain yourself when your trust is in Jesus. You do not have to do the fighting when you allow God to fight your battles for you.

124

SMA refused to bow, and they didn't burn. The same people who will ask you why you won't bow to the uncertainty, fear, and worry are the same people who will wonder in amazement at how you didn't burn.

You may not have ever realized it, but we are faced with the same decision that SMA had to make all the time. Will you bow to the uncertainty of the ending? Or will you put your trust in the one who controls the outcome?

I have a two year old nephew named Solomon. He might, quite literally, be the cutest kid I've ever seen. This sounds amazing right? A really cute nephew? It's the most amazing thing and terrifying thing at the same time. What if Maddy and I have ugly kids? What if our kids are ugly, and their cousin looks like he belongs on the *Pampers* commercials? That would be tragic.

I love Solomon so much. It's really cool right now for Maddy and I because we can borrow him for a few hours a day and give him back at night without any sort of sleep interruption. Incredible.

When we are with him we do all sorts of things. We play with fire trucks and kick soccer balls. We go swimming and eat goldfish. We eat LOTS of goldfish.

But you know what Solomon never, ever, does? He never pushes away his fire truck and asks me how his parents are going to pay the mortgage that month. He never stops kicking the soccer ball to see if we know how long it's going to take him to pay for his student loans. He's never once handed me back the goldfish bag and wondered if he'd ever get to eat them again.

And if he did...I'd think it was CRAZY. I'd be like bro...relax? Like, have a juice box or something, kid.

I think God has to feel the same way about us sometimes as he watches us running around in frantic little circles, worrying about the uncertain parts of our life. We're staying up wondering and worrying and, He's up in heaven like: "Woah. Relax. Have a juice box."

Why is it that we have no problem trusting God with our eternity, but it's so hard for us to trust him with Tuesday? We have faith for him to handle our *fate*, but we don't have faith for him to handle our *fire*.

God has it under control. He's never not had it under control. Believe it or not, He doesn't need your help at all. He wants to take the burden off of your shoulders so that you can simply enjoy being with him. Being a Christian is not asking Jesus to be your co-pilot; it's giving Him the steering wheel, strapping in and saying: "Where you want to take me I'm ready to go". Let him tell you where the destination is while you enjoy the journey.

There is *so* much peace in that. Even in the fire.

The peace of God does not look at your fire and leave you; the peace of God looks at your fire and covers you. If worry is a choice just as much as trust is, you might as well make the choice that allows you to have peace today.

Viral Jesus
@ViralJesus

The peace of God does not look at the fire and leave you. The peace of God looks at the fire and covers you.

In order for this to happen, we have to change the way we approach following Jesus altogether. I have heard thousands...no really, thousands of prayers start like this: "Lord please give me CLARITY regarding _____".

Lately, God has been convicting me about the things that I pray for. You see, a prayer for clarity is actually a prayer that makes it easier for us to not have to trust God. If we had clarity over every area in our life, why would we need to trust? Why would we need God at all in this life if we had it all under control?

See, God knows that the peace, hope, and life that you are so desperately looking for would not come if you had clarity. Clarity does not offer those things. Maybe for a moment, but it would come to an end. Only God can offer you those things for eternity. So he doesn't give you clarity - he gives you the opportunity to trust him, and through that, you get to experience all the blessings that come with being in his presence. Forever.

Psalms 23:1-4 says, "The Lord is my shepherd, I lack nothing. He makes me lie down in green pastures, He leads me beside quiet waters, He refreshes my soul. He guides me along the right paths for his name's sake. Even though I walk through the darkest valley, I will fear no evil, for you are with me."

A sheep doesn't need clarity. They just need a shepherd. You have one, and He's good at what he does. He refreshes your soul even in the darkest valleys of life, and those valleys become a lot less scary when you have the Light of the World walking right beside you.

The last words Jesus spoke on this earth bring me so much comfort:

"Behold. I am with you always." (Matthew 28:20)

Back to SMA for just a second. There's a tiny detail to their story we haven't covered that I believe will mean something to you. In Daniel 3, the Bible says that SMA were bound with rope and thrown into the fiery furnace of death. Not even lava boy could save them now.

So here's the sequence of events:

1.) They are bound/tied up/ put in chains.

2.) They trust Jesus anyways.

3.) Thrown into the fiery furnace of death.

4.) The only thing that gets burned are their chains.

Don't miss this. This is where it gets good.

Many times we can over spiritualize things when it comes to following Jesus. We are looking for our "breakthroughs" or our moments where the chains fall off. Don't get me wrong here, I'm not belittling those desires that may be in your heart. All I'm saying is - are we complicating that process?

Notice that SMA are *bound*. They trust Jesus, and then the very things that had them tied up are the only things that get burned. They went in the fire tied up. They went in the fire in chains. They went in the fire without their freedom. *They trusted Jesus*. Then: they came out of the fire free.They came out of the fire whole. They came out of the fire a miracle.

Could your breakthrough be as easy as trusting Jesus? Maybe you came into this chapter bound, but you are going to trust Jesus and leave it free. Maybe you came into this chapter empty, but you're going to leave it full of His hope. You came into today in chains, but you are leaving it with complete peace that only God can give you. You came into today feeling alone, but you are going to leave today knowing there is another man in the fire with you who you can TRUST.

Psalms 62:6 says, "Surely He is my rock and my salvation. I will not be shaken."

When it feels like you are close to hitting rock bottom: TRUST. Jesus will be your rock at the bottom. The same Jesus that loved you so much that He hung on a cross and died for you is the same Jesus who cares about your struggle today. He didn't do all that just to leave you. He's with you. He loves you. He's *for* you, and you can trust Him. Sometimes you just need a reminder that God hasn't forgotten about you. That He sees you. That He cares. This is that reminder.

Get back up and trust again.

When you put your trust in Jesus, the only thing that falls are the chains that bound you.

Trust. Fall.

Trust Fall.

winning in the wilderness

Matthew 4:1-11

Afterward, the Holy Spirit led Jesus into the lonely wilderness in order to reveal his strength against the accuser by going through the ordeal of testing. And after fasting for forty days, Jesus was extremely weak and famished. Then the tempter came to entice him to provide food by doing a miracle. So he said to Jesus, "How can you possibly be the Son of God and go hungry? Just order these stones to be turned into loaves of bread." He answered, "The Scriptures say: Bread alone will not satisfy, but true life is found in every word, which constantly goes forth from God's mouth." Then the accuser transported Jesus to the holy city of Jerusalem and perched him at the highest point of the temple and said to him, "If you're really God's Son, jump, and the angels will catch you. For it is written in the Scriptures: He will command his angels to protect you and they will lift you up so that you won't even bruise your foot on a rock." Once again Jesus said to him, "The Scriptures say:
You must never put the Lord your God to a test." And the third time the accuser lifted Jesus up into a very high mountain range and showed him all the kingdoms of the world and all the splendor that goes with it. "All of these kingdoms I will give to you," the accuser said, "if only you will kneel down before me and worship me." But Jesus said, "Go away, enemy! For the Scriptures say: Kneel before the Lord your God and worship only him." At once the accuser left him, and angels suddenly gathered around Jesus to minister to his needs.

If I'm honest, I think about germs way too much. I'm 100% a germaphobe. BIG hand sanitizer guy over here, OK?

Sometimes when I'm talking to people I will very intentionally avoid shaking their hand because I do not trust your hand sanitizing habits. Someone will go in for a handshake, and I come charging in with a quick side hug so I don't have to do any skin to skin contact. Judge me.

To this day, I'm the guy who uses those little toilet seat paper covers in public restrooms. You know what I'm talking about. They're basically like .2 inches of paper separating your butt from the seat, but to me those things are non-negotiable. I can remember so many times having to *really* use the bathroom, like sprinting in there, only to lay that flimsy piece of paper out gingerly so that it covered every corner of the toilet seat before I could sit.

I love traveling and I love airports. Recently I discovered that there is no worse place for a Germaphobe than an airplane. I had some time to kill in the airport one day so I walked into a bookstore. In the store, they had this little book of random airplane facts and one of them in particular caught my eye. It said that airplanes use "recycled air".
At the time, it didn't particularly jump off the page to me, I actually thought this was a pretty cool concept. Wow. Science. Ya know? Like, good job NASA! Do work son!

About an hour later, I was sitting in row 27C, floating through the clouds, and the guy sitting in 27B let out a massive belch. I mean, this thing caused turbulence. And not just that but it smelled. It was one of those burps. Immediately, all I could think about was how for the next two-and-a-half hours I was going to be breathing in his *Beefy Crunch Dorito,* and there was nothing I could do about it because of "recycled air".

This was an extremely dark time in my life.

I thought about this transition for a long time, and to be honest, I'm really proud of what I came up with: *If you follow Jesus long enough, you're going to find yourself in situations that stink.* Pretty good huh?

If you follow Jesus long enough, you are bound to follow him into tricky situations that will take some time to get out of. Sometimes a very real confirmation that you are truly following Jesus is if you have followed him right into the middle of a storm.
Before I was saved (and sometimes now when I've had too much caffeine) I listened to Lil Wayne. In one of his songs he said "Life is a beach, I'm just playing in the sand". Can I just be honest with you? Sometimes my life feels like it is the furthest thing from a beach. In fact, if I had to compare what my life feels like to a place sometimes, I would call it a wilderness.

The wilderness is a place that we absolutely will find ourselves in as followers of Jesus who are trying to go Viral for His purposes. The wilderness can manifest itself as all sorts of things in your life: Loneliness, waiting seasons, feeling far from God, temptation, losing people close to you, etc. The Wilderness could even be something going on that no one else is even aware of. You could have it all on the outside but feel lost on the inside. It is quite possible for your situation to be doing better than your soul.

The word "wilderness" is used over 300 times in the bible, and it presents itself in many forms and situations. The Israelites wandered in the wilderness for decades. Adam and Eve sinned in the wilderness. King David was hunted down by an angry and spiteful king in the wilderness.

But Jesus...He WON in the wilderness. I believe if we follow his example, we can win there, too.

The Wilderness could set you back in your quest for more of Jesus, or it could set you up to go viral in a way that you never thought possible.

If you want to thrive in the wilderness seasons of life, you're going to need food.

Matthew 4:4 Jesus said "It is written: Man shall not live on bread alone, but on every word that comes from the mouth of God." The devil would love for you to step into the wilderness on an empty stomach. He doesn't want you eating because he knows that eating works the same way spiritually as it does naturally. If you started skipping meals regularly, you'd become weak and small. When you start skipping out on God's Word, you become weak and small spiritually. You become an easy target for temptation. The devil doesn't even have to fight you when you aren't eating — eventually you are going to die on your own from spiritual starvation.

The other thing about being in the wilderness? Jesus knows the way out. And how can you follow Jesus when you do not even know what He says? You aren't even strong enough to follow at that point, let alone fight someone who "prowls around like a roaring lion" (1 Peter 5:8). If you want to fight against evil, if you want to follow the Guide out, you have to eat.

In the story of Jesus in the wilderness, we learn that even the devil knows scripture. He routinely tries to take scripture out of context and use it against God's people. My question for you is simple: does the devil know more Scripture than you?

I remember one time at our church a student accepted Jesus for the first time and someone gave him a Bible. The Bible translation was the Old King James Version, which doesn't exactly use the most relevant language. A few weeks went by and this student started coming into church saying things like: "Where art thou K-Cups for the coffee machine?" and he started sending out text messages like: "At what time shall ye arrive at thy father's house today?"

We all were like, "Bro! Somebody please get this man a message translation of the Bible or something!" But here's the thing; at least he was reading his Word. At least he was eating. At least he was not claiming to follow Jesus and then doing so blindly.

We have become way too dependent on other people feeding us. We read tweets about Jesus, listen to podcasts about Jesus, read other people's bible studies about Jesus, but how often do we go and spend time with Jesus for ourselves? We don't need to tweet; we need to EAT.

We are the most over-resourced and under-read generation ever when it comes to the Bible. At any time in our day we have access to some of the greatest sermons, podcasts, and videos on Earth. Those can be amazing additions to our relationship with God, but they cannot be the foundation of our relationship with God. We've been given a direct line of communication to the King of Kings and the Lord of Lords and we often settle for playing a game of telephone with Him. Instead of speaking to Him and listening to Him for ourselves, we settle for listening to what He has spoken to others. We have a second-hand faith when He called us to a first hand encounter. God wants to speak directly to you. Are you listening?

I have heard dozens and dozens of young people say a variation of this statement: "I just don't really get fed at my church".

I completely understand that it is possible to go to a church that does not meet your needs, but I feel confident in saying that there is a much higher chance that the church you go to fits your needs just fine, you are just relying too much on a pastor to feed you.

Can you imagine saying this statement regarding eating physically? Imagine you are a 21-year-old college student and your parents come into town to buy you some groceries. They stock your pantry *full* of the good stuff and then they head back out of town. What a blessing. Praise the Lord for his overflowing of *Cinnamon Toast Crunch* and *Cheetos*. Now imagine they leave and you start binge watching your favorite show on Netflix again like you were doing before they got there. You spend six hours watching, then ten hours and finally you are like "MAN. I'M HUNGRY. I wish somebody would come feed me. This really stinks. I'm just not getting fed like I should be. How come nobody will come and feed me?"

How ridiculous would that be? *Get yo lazy butt up and go get yourself some food out of the kitchen!*

You don't need somebody to feed you the word of God; you need to get up and go feed yourself. You don't need a waitress, the word of God is all-you-can-eat buffet and the food is hot and ready! You are not truly serious about going viral for Jesus, winning in the wilderness, or your calling until you are first serious about getting in the word of God for yourself.

Viral Jesus
@ViralJesus

You are not truly serious about going viral for Jesus, winning in the wilderness, or your calling until you are first serious about getting in the word of God for yourself.

The entire time Jesus was in the wilderness he fought by saying, "It is written".
When the world tries to tell you that you're less than, you need to be able to say: "Psalms 139:14 I am fearfully and wonderfully made."

When you feel surrounded you need to declare: "Exodus 14:14, The Lord will fight for me, I just need to be still"

When you're in pain you need to remember Romans 8:18: "The pain that you've been feeling, can't compare to the joy that is coming."

When you're afraid, you need to remember what Isaiah 41:10 says: "So do not fear for I am with you."

No matter what kind of attack the enemy tries to throw your way, you've been given a weapon that can overcome all of it: the unshakeable Word of God!

My wife Maddy and I have been married for one year. It's been absolutely amazing. Sure we've had moments where things have been tough, but we are learning so much, and it's been a year that I will always look back on and be so thankful for.

In our first year of marriage, I've learned the discipline of effort. A great relationship takes effort. For instance: if I come home from work and choose to ignore the dishes in the sink, allow the dirty clothes hamper to overflow with dirty socks, and expect Maddy to take the dog for a walk...chances are, that night is not going to end well for me.

BUT, if I come home and look for ways to help around the house without Maddy asking me, intentionally create moments for quality time between the two of us and ask her questions about her day...that normally leads to a *great* night. Yeah, marriage rules.

One of the biggest keys in any good relationship is effort. "Christianity is a relationship not a religion" is a very popular thing to quote. Because it's true. But I've found that many people who say this phrase would have horrible relationships if they treated all of their relationships the way they treat the one they have with Jesus, because there's no effort put forth! A great relationship requires effort from both sides. Jesus is putting forth effort every day, but it takes two to tango.

I'm not saying you have to earn it with Jesus. That's the opposite of the Gospel. We are saved by grace and grace alone. But grace is not the enemy of effort, it's the enemy of earning. We don't have to try and pay for our sins (thank goodness, because we could never afford the cost). But we do have to intentionally put effort into our relationship with Jesus if we want to become more like Him and survive our wilderness seasons. In fact, we were created not just to survive but to thrive.

Intimacy with Jesus leads to authority in the wilderness.

One of the biggest ways we can put forth effort in our relationship with Jesus is through our quiet time with the Lord.

When I was 21-years-old, I started a Bible Study in my apartment. I didn't have many intentions for this bible study other than having a few friends over to grow in intimacy with Jesus. But God had other plans. Within a few short months we had grown in size from nine people to over one hundred. By the end of that same year, we had over four hundred young adults gathering on a weekly basis to worship the name of Jesus. Now, you might think: *Wow Noah, that had to be so awesome! I bet you were so pumped to see that happen!*

But the truth is, I was terrified. I was terrified that people were going to get too close to me and see that I wasn't that great of a leader. I was afraid that if people realized that I was just a normal 21-year-old trying to lead hundreds of people the same age as me, that the whole ministry would fall apart. I had this ridiculous insecurity that I needed to become someone who I *was not* instead of focusing on who Jesus *was*.

One morning, in my quiet time, I got real with God. I remember praying out loud for God to relieve me from the pressure that I felt like I was under. I was exhausted from playing the game and always feeling like I had to be "on" in front of the people around me. That morning, God spoke something to me that has since changed my life forever.

He said: *Noah, if you want to lead these people you have to be willing to go somewhere they haven't been. Bury yourself so deep inside of my presence that when people interact with you they'll be able to see Me and not you. It's not about the words you come up with; it's about the well that you dig. Dig deep.*

Ever since that day, the pressure has been taken off. My focus has been to go deeper with Jesus, and through that process, I've learned that I don't have to be anything special. In fact, God gets more glory working through ordinary people who have to believe in God to do something special than He does "perfect" people who seem to have it all figured out. God doesn't need you to do miracles or multiply fish for thousands of people; He just needs you to go deeper with Him and trust Him with your fish sticks.

It breaks my heart when I see young Christian leaders sacrifice intimacy with Jesus for things that do not mean anything. You can be famous on Earth, but unknown in Heaven. God wants you to be famous in Heaven so that you can be effective on Earth.

Your anointing doesn't come from a platform it comes from a person. It's one thing to do things in His name, but it's another to know the person behind the name. That's where real power and influence resides. If you want to make a true impact for Jesus, you have to go deep and let God take you wide.

Remember the story of Daniel? He had more influence in his prayer closet than the king of the country did on his throne. If you chase influence with people, your impact will always be limited. But when you chase intimacy with Jesus, you will be anointed and favored to stand in front of kings and queens. We need more prayer closets and less thrones.

Jesus is not looking for the most influential people in our generation - He's looking for the ones He can trust to go viral with His message.

A huge part of following Jesus is relying on the Holy Spirit to guide you. Maybe you have PTSD from the words "Holy Spirit" like I did. There's a good chance you associate the person of the Holy Spirit with some really crazy stuff you've seen in church that you aren't quite sure how you feel about. But the Holy Spirit is not weird; people are weird. Many people look at The Holy Spirit as someone who gives goosebumps instead of what He truly does: gives power. God sent the Holy Spirit to us as a gift. Its' role in our lives is to reveal Jesus to us, to further the Kingdom of God on this earth, to comfort us, and strengthen us so we can get out of the wilderness.

The Holy Spirit is not a feeling; it's a filling.
What the enemy would love for us to believe is that we don't need the power of The Holy Spirit working in our lives. He wants you to think that because you saw The Holy Spirit abused in a church service it gives you the right to avoid it. Because the devil knows that when we avoid the Holy Spirit, we become void of the power it offers us as Jesus followers.

When Jesus won in the wilderness He won because of two things. 1. The word of God and 2. The spirit of God living inside of him. If you want to win in the wilderness, you'll need the same things.

The Word + The Spirit = The Win.

We need reinforcements. You cannot fight temptation on a daily basis on your own. You stand no match making it through the hard seasons of life with will power or discipline. We desperately need the Holy Spirit and the only thing you have to do to have it is ask.

If you really want to leave a mark on this earth through your life, it's time to get real about the things that matter.

I challenge you to seek the face of God more than you seek the faces of followers.

I challenge you to ask for the Holy Spirit more than you ask for advice from others.

I challenge you to know God's word better than you do your favorite preacher's sermons.

I challenge you to go deeper instead of going wider.

You were made to win in the wilderness.

Go win.

The Share

friends

The Share.

It's impossible to go viral if your life isn't shared. This section shows you how to make an impact much larger than you could possibly imagine. This section builds on your plan and your post and gives a blueprint for sharing what's taken place inside of you with the world. The share is the part of the book dedicated to crowding Heaven.

Ecclesiastes 4:9-10 "Two are better than one, because they have a good return for their labor. If either one of them falls down, one can help the other up. But pity anyone who falls and has no one to help them up."

I really wish I was tough enough to be a Navy Seal. I wish I had the anchor tattoo on my left bicep, and the super cool camo pants that they tuck into their desert camo boots. I love watching movies about those guys. They are bad to the bone.

But what really stands out to me about Navy Seals is their unity. Recently our world has experienced all sorts of division. Everything from racial division, economic division, political division... the list goes on forever. I've watched as our world has been dismantled seemingly overnight, all because of disagreements and extreme disunity. When I watch the Navy Seals in action, they are the exact opposite. They are the epitome of unity.

I recently watched an interview of a former Navy Seals Commander explaining the unity of the Seal teams. His answer was profound to me: "Unity isn't just important. Unity is survival. Every day we step into a mission that is life or death — if you can't trust the person beside you when you do that you are toast. Skin color, political preference, background... none of those things matter when lives are in the balance. Unity is survival."

By no means am I trying to dramatize or belittle the incredible things our armed forces do for us on a daily basis when I say this: but we are on a mission that is the difference between life and death.

Taking the Gospel of Jesus Christ to the world is a mission far too big for us to do on our own; People's entire eternities are at stake. This mission is too critical for us to let disagreements stop it. An important mission needs a unified team. If the mission is worth dying for; the people on your team are worth loving.

Just before Jesus was arrested and taken to the cross to be crucified, He prayed one last prayer for the future Church. His prayer was not for wisdom, it was not for great church strategy, or for resources — His last prayer for us was for unity. Jesus knew that the greatest threat to our mission as the body of Christ was disunity.

This mission is too big to do alone. This fight is hard enough without us fighting each other. You need a team to have your back. You need a team to fight with you who doesn't see you as anything less than what we all are: Sons and Daughters of Christ, who are all at equal height at the foot of the cross.

Take David.

You know the story: just your average young shepherd boy out in a field killing lions and bears with his bare hands. You know, just chilling. Some random old guy shows up at his house and tells him he is going to be king. A short time later he kills a ten-foot-tall guy with massive biceps using a slingshot. Then he gets taken to the palace to serve a crazy, delusional, mad scientist kind of King. He stays in that palace for years and goes through a crazy hard time of fighting wars and dodging death threats and spears (his story is insane just go read it all in 1 Samuel —you'll love it. It's got all the drama. A real Netflix show before Netflix). But finally, years after he was anointed to be the next King of Israel, it became time for Him to step into that role. But it was extremely tricky to say the least since the crazy King was still in power and had no intention of giving up his throne. David was going to need God to intervene in a big way to make it happen. God, who is always faithful to come through, intervenes and sends David a friend named Jonathan.

I find it so interesting that when David's time had come for him to step fully into his calling God did not send him an army, a bunch of money, or some massive platform. God sent him a friend.

Viral Jesus
@ViralJesus

When David's time had come for him to step fully into his calling God did not send him an army, a bunch of money, or some massive platform. God sent him a friend.

For you, it will probably be the same.

The number one way God influences your life is through your relationships. The number one way the devil influences your life also happens to be through your relationships. So yes, your squad is extremely important.

If you want to go Viral for Jesus - if you truly want to take what God has done for you and let God begin to work through you, it is absolutely vital that you have friends who are not only on the same team as you, but running beside you on the same mission.

You don't need hype-men or hype-women. You need brothers and sisters in Christ who care enough to have your back in prayer. You need friends who aren't afraid to speak up when they see you falling short. You need people in your life that care more about the mission and calling that God has placed on your life than they do popularity or opinion.

I am not saying to cut-off your friendships that are with people who don't follow Jesus. That's not the point at all. Jesus was literally called the "friend of sinners". I'm just saying to make sure that your inner-circle is a unified team. This mission is too critical for it to be anything else.

At the time I'm writing this book I've been following Jesus for about five years. I've been in vocational ministry for four of those years. In that time, I have watched as leader after leader, Christian after Christian, has fallen down and made horrible mistakes and compromises. I've seen pastors cheat on their wives. I've seen mothers get hooked on drugs. I've seen people take money from the church. I've seen horrible mistakes happen from people I never would have dreamed of seeing fall.

What I've realized is that those people didn't wake up one day and say, "today's the day I'm going to cheat on my wife". Or "today's the day I'm going to make a massive mistake that will possibly ruin my life". It started with small things.

A seed of compromise always starts small. But eventually, it will strangle you.

In almost all of the cases I mentioned above, compromise started at the same time that a lack of accountability did. The devil loves to isolate people because he knows our mission is too big to be a solo one. He knows that you are ten times more likely to make small compromises when there is no one watching your back.

Don't fall for it. It's a trap.

Accountability stinks in the short-term but it can save your life in the long-term. Your calling is too important and your role is too big for you to let something like a seed of compromise bury itself in your garden.

Grab a few friends and dig your heels in together. Get real with one another. Don't act like everything is fine when it isn't. Confess your sin and your struggles to one another so that you can have each other's back and hold each other accountable. It's not easy and it can be awkward. But I would rather go through some awkward conversations so that I could fulfill the calling God has placed on my life than be afraid of conversations and die from compromise before I ever went Viral for Jesus.

This mission is too important for you not to care who is on it with you.

There's a famous quote that says, "Show me your five closest friends, and I'll show you your future."

That quote is fire. But I'd like to take it a step further because in the Kingdom of God your future is not just about you.

Show me your five closest friends, and I'll show you the success or failure of your calling.
Show me your five closest friends, and I'll show you the success or failure of reaching a generation for the Gospel of Jesus.
Show me your five closest friends, and I'll show you a mess or a miracle.

Show me your five closest friends and I'll show you mission failure or mission complete.

when your calling gets cloudy

Every Summer when I was a kid, my family went to Myrtle Beach for vacation. It was awesome. So many valuable life lessons were learned on that beach. I learned to surf there. I learned how to make friends with strangers there. Myrtle Beach is where I learned that seagulls were evil, evil creatures. For real. One of them attacked me for my hotdog one time while it was halfway in my mouth.

His name was Jeffrey and we are NOT on speaking terms.

One year on our annual family vacation I remember the weather being less than ideal the entire week we were there. Storms came and went, which made our beach time less than normal and our sun tans not quite as dark. The day after we were supposed to leave, there was actually a tropical storm coming through.

Because of the weather, the water was extremely dangerous. The waves there were already pretty big, but this week they were treacherous.

Being the man of the family, and by man I mean the oldest of the cousins (13 at the time) with the tiniest hint of chest hair, I was asked to help make sure no one went too far out into the water. All of our parents were paying good attention to us, but they knew I was a good swimmer and wanted me to help them keep watch.

I took this request...this job...this *duty*, very serious.

I felt like Larry the Lifeguard Lobster from *Spongebob* (if you don't know what I'm talking about just know I had a moment of silence for you as I was writing this). I remember pulling my shoulders back, puffing my chest out and surveying the beach like I was a marine on patrol fighting for his country.

After all, my aunts and uncles...my parents, they trusted me. They saw something in me. They knew I was the man for this job.

I took this responsibility so seriously that I literally sat down my five cousins and gave them a speech before they got in the water. I'll save you the manuscript of the speech for the sake of time, but just know that it was extremely inspirational and only one of my younger cousins picked his nose as I was giving it. It was *that* good.

A few minutes later everyone ran off into the water and I felt like the absolute man. I felt like I had it all under control. For about five minutes.

That's when I realized I was not Larry the lifeguard.

I looked up from building sand castles to observe my flock. To my horror, all I could see of my little sister and my cousin Lexy was their heads bobbing up and down in the water to my left. They had absolutely no regard for my rules. They didn't respect me. They didn't even care! And more importantly, they were not safe!

I started waving and yelling at them to come back towards the shore but they couldn't hear me due to the sound of crashing waves. They looked back at me and must have thought I was dancing because they started doing the Y-M-C-A signs back to me as they sang out the melody of the famous song.

I could not believe what was happening.

I looked to my right only to be more discouraged. The oldest girl, Taylor, was out just as far in the water. Only, she had an iced vanilla latte from Starbucks in her right hand (she obviously did not care about the turtles then, but I would like to inform you that she has since found the Lord and cares much more deeply about the Lord's creation). Taylor was waving too. But Taylor was ignoring rule number one when it comes to swimming in the ocean: never turn your back on the waves. As a matter of fact, there are only two things you should never turn your back on: your wife when she is shopping at *Target*, and the ocean. As she was waving to me to come join her in the water, a massive wave crashed down on her from behind, burying her and her overpriced coffee into the sea.

154

I stood on the shore looking to my left and to my right, a shiver of helplessness surging throughout my body as I remember thinking: maybe the adults picked the wrong person for the job.

Maybe I wasn't called to be a lifeguard at all.

The thing I had just minutes before been so confident in I was now questioning. I went from being excited to being discouraged.

My calling went from being clear to being cloudy.

Have you ever felt like your calling went from clear to cloudy?

Maybe at some point in your life it was crystal clear. You knew exactly what you were meant to do with your life. You had a seven-step plan and pocket full of sunshine. You knew what classes you would need to take, how much money you were going to make, and you finally felt like you knew what your purpose was in life.

But then, something happened.

Maybe life hit you in the mouth unexpectedly. Maybe finances made it unlikely that you'd be able to go to school for what you wanted to do. Maybe you just didn't think you were very good in that area of life after all.

Your calling was so clear....but then it went cloudy.

Or maybe your calling has always been cloudy. You listened to my story about being a lifeguard and you related much more to my cousin with the *Starbucks* in her hand who got crushed by the waves.

If you relate to anything that I'm saying — join the club.

I would say that over half of the coffee shop conversations I have (there are a lot of those) are about calling. Everyone wants to know what theirs is. Everyone wants to know their purpose. We all desire to find the meaning that our life can bring to the world... If only there was a way to make our cloudy callings clear again.

As a follower or apprentice of Jesus, your first calling is simple. It's the same calling as me: love God & love people.

Chances are, you're reading this book out of some desire to do one of those two things better. You probably already desire to go deeper in your relationship with God. You already know that you're supposed to love people. You're trying really hard to love your college roommate who refuses to wash her dishes that she leaves in the sink. Every time you walk in the kitchen you want to throw a pan, but instead, you take a deep breath and think "Love God. Love people".

That's awesome. You're better than I am. I'm a pan thrower.

Our first calling of loving God and loving people is simple. That does not make it easy; but it's simple nonetheless.

It's the *other* calling that's complicated.

The calling that's more individualized is the one that we tend to struggle making clear in our lives. What am I actually good at? What do I do that gives me purpose? How can I make a living and still do *that*?

The problem with these questions is that many times our answers to them change. We find out we're not as good at that thing as we thought we were. We stop finding purpose in what once gave us purpose before. Maybe the thing you thought was your calling doesn't pay you as well as you thought it would, and you've decided that having enough money to raise a family is much more important to you now that you're married.

Here's the thing: Your calling can change.

This was actually a life changing realization for me. I realized that when I took the pressure off of myself to find my "destination" calling or job, it allowed me to enjoy the journey of following Jesus so much more.

Psalms 37:23 says, "The steps of a righteous person are ordered and they *delight* in their way".

Jesus orders our steps, but he often doesn't tell us where the next step is going to be until it's time to take it. Why? Because when you don't know where the destination is you have to trust in the one telling you where to step. The more you trust in Jesus, the more you find *delight* in Him. The more you trust in Jesus, the more joy you have on the journey.

If Jesus gave you all of your life's steps up front, you wouldn't have to trust in anybody. You'd miss out on so much of the delight in following Jesus. You'd miss out on the adventure of following Jesus. That's an adventure you do not want to miss for a second...not even a step.

Maybe the question is not: "What's my calling?"

But rather: "How do I become someone who lives like they are called?"

If your calling feels cloudy or if you are stressed about the next step in your life, I'm going to give you three things to check. If you check these three things I can personally *guarantee* you that your calling will come back into focus (I sound like a guy on a tv commercial selling you cleaning products). Why is this important? Because when you live out the calling on your life, it affects everyone around you. You share Jesus not just through your words but through your obedience. So let's check these 3 things:

1.) Check your cheers.

Don't check who is cheering *for* you. Check who you are cheering *for*. Is it hard for you to cheer for other people? Is it hard for you to cheer for people who are more successful than you are? Is it hard for you to cheer for people who do the same thing as you?

If you can't cheer for other people, chances are you have sacrificed your calling for a competition.

When Jesus was walking around on earth, He had these 12 guys who followed Him everywhere. They were called His disciples. They got to walk with Jesus, talk with Jesus, watch Jesus perform miracles, and be taught by Jesus in human form. How cool is that? I'm not jealous, you're jealous.

Jesus hand picked these 12 guys to follow him. He "called" them. Can you imagine the honor they must have felt in that moment? Thousands of people in their city and Jesus chose...them? He didn't just choose them; He chose them for THIS.

If there was any hesitation in the 12 when Jesus called them, I don't know where it would have come from. This was the opportunity of a lifetime. They were *called*. They were *chosen*.

But fast forward just a few short months later: the disciples are sitting around at their version of a Chick-Fil-A eating lunch and they ask Jesus: "Who is the greatest out of us?" and "Who is going to do the greatest things for you?"

Wait — what? In just a short amount of time, everything flipped upside down. They are sitting next to Jesus, they have an amazing calling, but all they can do is COMPETE?

Check your cheers. If you can't cheer, you're competing, and that affects your calling.

Growing up in our neighborhood, the ice cream truck came every Saturday morning. I loved ice cream. OK, I still love ice cream. OK, I literally scream for ice cream.

Every Saturday morning I would play in my room with the curtains completely open so that I could keep watch for the ice cream truck. One Saturday morning when I was pretty young, I heard the noise of the truck's music blaring before I even saw it's beautiful sight. I ran into the living room screaming that the ice cream truck was coming and I needed money ASAP. My mom hurried into her bedroom to retrieve some cash.

How I wish life still worked that way.

I remember impatiently waiting as I looked out the window at the truck. I watched as my friend, a young boy only a year older than me who lived across the street from us named Troy, was already in line receiving his ice cream cone. That day, I had my first encounter with bitterness. It should be ME standing out there with an ice cream cone right now. Troy's mom was faster and it wasn't fair! Look at Troy the way he's eating that ice cream cone, he thinks he is big stuff. He's not big stuff at all. I bet he doesn't even know how to tie his shoes by himself yet like me.

Finally my mom handed me a five dollar bill and I ran outside. I was so jealous and so bitter that I ordered TWO ice cream cones just in the hopes that Troy, who didn't even know I had been watching him, would see me enjoying more ice cream than he got. That would surely show him (it would also be my downfall when my mom realized I spent $2 instead of $1 without her permission just a few minutes later).

You might be listening to this story thinking: *man, Noah, you've got problems. You seriously thought like that as a kid? I'm gonna pray for YOU.* Yes. Please do!

This is exactly what we do with our callings when we start to compare. We let bitterness and jealousy stir up in our heart and it affects how we view ourselves and our own calling. We start doing things not because Jesus told us to do them, but because we want to prove ourselves to others around us. We want to be the best. We want to impress. We want to be cheered for. Without even noticing it, we become people who are so hardened by the trap of comparison that we can no longer follow Jesus without taking detours to compete with those around us.

When you make your calling a competition with other people, you are actually taking the glory away from God and trying to give it to yourself. When you truly want God to receive the glory, you stop caring about credit. As long as HIS name is being glorified, you should just be looking for a way to help. Collaboration is so much more powerful than competition.

If your neighbor is blessed, that just means that God is in the neighborhood.

Viral Jesus
@ViralJesus

If your neighbor is blessed, that just means that God is in the neighborhood.

If your neighbor is being used, that just means that God is in the neighborhood. The neighborhood is the kingdom of God. The cool part about that neighborhood is that when my neighbor wins, I actually win too. Because in the kingdom of God we are not trying to go viral for our name's sake, we are doing it for the name that saved us from our sin. We are after making the name of JESUS famous, not our own.

So if your neighbor starts "winning", ask how you can help them. When you do that, you are actually helping the kingdom of God advance on this earth and you are beginning to look more and more like Jesus.

Don't let your calling be another casualty of comparison. How can we love our enemies like Jesus commands us to do when we can't even love our friends? Our God is too good for that. His kingdom is too grand for that. I'm rooting for you. I'm cheering for you. Check your cheers.

2.) Check your Service.

Who are you serving?

We all want our lives to count for something. We want our lives to have purpose. We want it all to mean something. That's a good thing. However, what the world says "means something" is very different from what Jesus says "means something". Worldly success is fleeting. It's here today and gone tomorrow. Worldly success is confined to you as an individual, and that's fool's gold. This is why we see celebrities and many others who achieve amazing things and have everything the world has to offer, still hit rock bottom. So many times when people reach the world's highest peaks is when they also feel the lowest.

People grind their entire lives to achieve certain levels of fame, money, and success. Then they get it and they say things like, "I wish I would have spent more time with the people I love," or "It still feels empty".

Maybe the grind lied to us?

This grind has even crept into the Church. We become so focused on doing *for* God that we completely forget to be *with* God. We are too busy with our callings.

Have you noticed how many sermons are preached on calling? Have you noticed how many sermons lately there are on your destiny or the future blessings you are going to get? The destiny gospel has become the new prosperity gospel!

It's led to an entire generation of Jesus followers waiting on destiny to show up instead of enjoying their God who already has.

We celebrate the ones who have already achieved this "destiny". The famous pastors, the influencers and the people on stage. Wow, look at them! I love those people. Shoot, I stand on stages and talk about Jesus pretty regularly. But this is not the goal. Jesus is the goal.

If we celebrate people who hold microphones more than we do the people who hold the doors, we've got the message of Jesus completely twisted! It's easy sometimes to think of Jesus as some traveling rockstar preacher who went from stadium to stadium preaching hot fire. The reality is that Jesus only spoke to large crowds a handful of times in his life. The rest of the time? He was serving others. He was washing people's feet. He was loving His neighbor. Chances are, if Jesus came to your church, He'd be holding the door not the microphone.

What is celebrated is popularized, but we don't celebrate door holders well enough. We celebrate the stage. This has put crazy amounts of desire in young people around the world to be the next great preacher or worship leader. Why? Because that's where the influence is! That's where the "big" calling is. Listen to me: That. Is. Some. Horse. Poop.

Influence is not found in being seen, it's found in being obedient.

Going viral in the kingdom of God is not about how many followers you have. It's about the kind of follower you are.

If you want to make the greatest possible impact on this world, don't try and build a platform — build a life following Jesus. Don't try and figure it all out right now. Just say yes to him today and take another step.

Who are you serving?

When I started following Jesus, everything about my life began to change. I was 21 years old when I gave my life to Christ.

At that time I was pretty big into photography. Not just any type of photography, but adventure photography. Ok I'll say it: #exploreandwander.

I was that guy.

In college I would drive all over the country on the weekends with my friends taking pictures on the side of mountain tops, next to some of the most beautiful stretches of beaches, and just about any city with a cool sunset view. And I got good at it. People started following me online to see my photos. Slowly but surely companies began to notice my work. Then one day I scored big time.

I received an email from someone in marketing at *Urban Outfitters*, a clothing store I loved shopping at but couldn't really afford (balling on a budget life, you feel me?). They had noticed my photos and wanted to work with me. ME!?

They said they would start paying me monthly and even send me a couple of boxes of free clothes every time I needed new stuff to shoot in. This was my dream!! I said yes immediately.

I started posting for *Urban Outfitters* and I felt like I had made it. I wasn't getting paid bank or anything, but I had awesome clothes and I was able to afford my steady diet of *Chick-Fil-A* with no problem.

At the same time, God started stirring things up in my heart. Thousands of people were interacting with my photos online and I started thinking about what it would be like to try and share Jesus with them. No...I couldn't do that. That's not what had built my platform. People wouldn't stick around for that. What would *Urban Outfitters* think? I had bills to pay! I had chicken sandwiches to buy!

One night I broke.

Earlier that day I had posted a photo for *Urban Outfitters*. My rep with the company had emailed me saying they wanted to renew my contract for another six months. They loved what I was doing. I'll never forget reading that email at the same time that the Holy Spirit put it on my heart to share about the grace of God on my *instagram*.

I picked up my phone and I uploaded a photo to my *instagram* of me on the side of a mountain. Only this time, instead of a caption about clothes or adventure, I shared the greatest adventure of my life: Following Jesus. I talked about where I had been when Jesus found me in my mess. I told people that the grace of God will find you no matter how far gone you may feel or seem to be — there was still hope! I pressed upload and turned my phone off.

That night I got a phone call from a photography friend who said I was a fool. This was surely going to ruin my working relationship with *Urban Outfitters,* he said. He told me I should delete it.

I didn't.

That night I lost almost 800 of my 6000 followers on Instagram. My prideful side kicked in and told me I should delete it.

I didn't.

Twenty-four hours later I got a message from a girl in Canada. She told me she had been following me online for several months because of my photos. She said she was surprised to see such a long caption on my recent post. She read the entire thing and longed to know more about this Jesus guy I was talking about with such passion. That same night she began surfing *YouTube* for more information and ended up giving her life to Christ. All because of an instagram caption I wanted desperately to delete.

I didn't know it at the time, but that night was a defining moment in my journey following Jesus. It was the beginning of me no longer trying to serve MY kingdom but truly serving HIS. For the first time in my life it wasn't about my name but His. Success had a different meaning to me.

What did it matter if I had a bunch of followers if I wasn't taking them anywhere worth going?

People thought I was crazy. Friends thought I had lost my mind. Shoot, some days I agreed with them. It kind of felt like I was losing my life. Then I read Matthew 10:39: "Whoever finds their life will lose it, and whoever loses their life for my sake will find it."

I was losing my life, but in the process I found life unlike anything I had experienced before. In fact, it's been a few years since I gave my life to Jesus now and I've been trying to lose my life ever since. Because the more I trade my desires for His, the more life I find.

Since that night I lost 800 followers (and more than a couple of friends), God has been so faithful. My online platform began to boom as I continued to share about Jesus. Within a few months thousands of new followers were coming to my page — not for my photos. but to hear about Jesus! I thought that my chances of working with any other companies online were completely ruined. But by the end of that same year, I had been hired by *Pacsun*, *Forever 21*, *Iams Dog Food* and I even got to renew that contract with *Urban Outfitters*.

When God asks you to do something that seems crazy to everybody else, He tends to have your back. When you're willing to give God all the pieces of the puzzle, you put yourself in position for God to put it together.

Pro Tip: God is a lot better at puzzles than you are.

Who are you serving? Whose kingdom are you building?

3.) Check Your Chase.

My greatest fear for our generation is that we will chase our callings more than we chase Christ. Did you know your calling could actually become an idol?

Humor me for a second.

If you're single, imagine your dream girl or dream guy for a second (if you're married imagine your spouse!!). Imagine you get to marry that Hillsong singing Beyonce or Harry Styles. The wedding is amazing. You even invited me because you read my book and wanted me to get to eat your wedding cake. You are so nice.

You and your dream spouse get in the car and you take him/her straight home. You help them unload all of their things in the house and you tell them goodnight and that you'll see them in a few days, maybe a week or so. You are so thankful you finally found them, BUT you've got a ton of work you need to do to make sure your marriage is awesome. You've got a bunch of money to make so that you guys can enjoy the rest of your marriage later. You've got a bunch of dreams and goals to accomplish so life is better later, so you bought a second house to sleep in so that you could stay focused on them better. Don't worry though! You'll be back soon to spend a few hours together and it's going to be awesome. Maybe you guys can even take a few photos together so everyone knows you're still together!

Whattttt?

Insane. This would never work in a marriage — so why do we try and make it work in our relationship with God?

We say that Jesus is going to be our prize in heaven but we live differently on earth.

We have access to GOD. The creator of the universe. The king of Kings and Lord of Lords. The one who made it possible for us to eat warm chocolate chip cookies with a cold glass of milk! The one who is unlike any other on this earth or above!

We jump into a relationship with Jesus and then we leave him at the house across the street so we can go focus on our goals. We have to go live out our callings! They are too important!

It may shock you when I say this, but it is very possible that your calling can keep you from Jesus. Jesus did not die on a cross for you so that you would do great things. He died on a cross for you because he wanted to be *with* you. Since you couldn't stop sinning, He came down and lived Holy and righteously for you. So He could be with you. Jesus wants sons and daughters not employees. So don't pimp out Jesus for your goals. Don't focus more on your dream than your king. Stop waiting to receive the prize when you have access to Him!

You want to make sure you don't miss out on your calling? Focus on the one who called, spend time with the one who called, make the one who called your heart's desire and you will not miss your calling. When you have a great relationship with God you do great things out of an overflow. You do great things because you are in relationship with a great God who cannot help Himself but to overflow into you.

Check your cheers. Check your service. Check your chase. If these three things are where they should be, your calling will begin to focus again in your life.

I've been around some people who've done some great things. I've been in rooms with the most famous pastors, some of the greatest leaders, and some celebrities who I follow on *Instagram*, and I'm not going to lie to you: I've fanboyed a little bit here and there.

But when we get to heaven I can guarantee you that is not going to happen. Nobody is going to be looking around going:

"OHH look! It's TD Jakes over there!!"

or

"OHHH man! It's Kanye West! He made it! I told you it was real, Aunt Susie! You should have stayed off Facebook!"

No one is going to be doing stuff like that in heaven. We aren't going to be concerned with who is to our left or right because we will be so awestruck by our King standing in front of us. His glory will be right in front of us and we will be in awe.

We'll be looking at the one

gives peace in the storm.
gives hope where there is none.
gives life today & eternally.
goes before you and behind you.
death bows to.
Who's beside you when you are all alone.
Who is above every other.

We will be looking at HIM. He's the one.

But He's here now. Our prize is available to us today. Right where you are.

When your calling gets cloudy, go back to your king.

into the night

Matthew 5:14-16 (MSG): "Here's another way to put it: You're here to be light, bringing out the God-colors in the world. God is not a secret to be kept. We're going public with this, as public as a city on a hill. If I make you light-bearers, you don't think I'm going to hide you under a bucket, do you? I'm putting you on a light stand. Now that I've put you there on a hilltop, on a light stand—shine! Keep an open house; be generous with your lives. By opening up to others, you'll prompt people to open up with God, this generous Father in heaven."

Have you thought you were going to be something or do something in your life, only to be sorely mistaken?

Maybe you watched a couple episodes of a *Food Network* show and thought that you were going to be an incredible cook. Then you burnt the *Toaster Strudels*. You can't even cook on an *Easy Bake Oven*. Maybe when you graduated high school you thought *I'm going to get a 4.0 in college*. An aspirational goal for sure. Then the second week of Freshmen year hits you and you try to drop out and get your money back. "Mom, I'm going to be an entrepreneur!"

When I was in the 9th grade, I truly thought I was going to be a professional rapper. Not like Wrapping gifts, like a rapper who raps to the beat.

Don't laugh.

I was like a jail cell back in the day — I had bars.

Maybe you're reading this and thinking: *I could see that Noah*. And to you I'd like to say thank you. If you're reading this and making fun of me, I'd like to say that you smell a lot like the Pharisees from the Bible.

OK too far!

I was in the 9th grade, I had 5th grade PE class. We were outside playing some basketball when one of my friends came up with the idea of having a "freestyle" rap battle, which basically just means, you come up with what you are going to say in the moment.

My opponent's name was Shawn. Shawn stood about five foot, nine inches tall, he was an above average basketball player, and he had a mustache that was extremely impressive for a kid his age. I knew this was going to be a tough battle.

Someone picked up a pencil and started using it like a drum stick to lay down a beat for us to rap over. Warning, it's about to get graphic. This was Shawn's line:

"Yo momma so fat she sat on a Home Depot and made it a Lowes."

Whatttt? Like first of all it didn't even rhyme but second of all don't talk about my momma or we gonna have problems.

The other guys watching and listening to our rap battle went crazy: "Ohhhhhhhh GOT EM"

I took a deep breath. I let the magic fly. I said: "Haters make me famous...I got my face on a cookie like Amos."

Gold.

I thought I had just set the basketball court on fire with that line. My friends were jumping up and down while I was just standing there with my head tilted sideways as I looked at Shawn like, why did you even try to take me on bro? You KNEW not to play with me with these bars.

Unfortunately, my rapping career never quite made it. I realized rather quickly that I did not, in fact, have any good bars and I definitely couldn't rap. But I've always still really enjoyed listening to it.

In 2012, Jay-Z released a song that would end up becoming one of his most popular hits ever. It was downloaded 10's of millions of times in just a matter of weeks. The song was called "No Church in the Wild". The entire message of the song was that the world was too wild for the church. The verses listed "wild" things one after the other and the chorus continued repeating "no church in the wild".

I look back now on that song and I actually agree with Jay-Z on part of his song. The world IS wild. Pandemics, mass shootings, racism, hate crimes, terrorism, drug addictions, poverty, pornography, sex trafficking, suicide...the list goes on and on. We live in a world that has never been more "wild".

While I agree with Jay-Z about the craziness of our world, I wholeheartedly disagree about the Church's role in it.

I don't think the Church is going to die in the wild, I think it's going to thrive.

Yes, we live in a dark, wild world... but darkness is where light shines the brightest. So, darkness is not just our greatest opposition but it's also our greatest opportunity.

Viral Jesus
@ViralJesus

Darkness is where light shines the brightest. So, darkness is not just our greatest opposition but it's also our greatest opportunity.

Have you ever tried to use a flashlight in the daytime? You can't even tell if it's on unless you cup your hand over it or stare directly into the bulb. But when it's the middle of the night, and you can't see the coffee table in front of you on your way to retrieve a midnight snack, a flashlight works wonderfully.
Our world is dark. But Jesus says, "you are here to be light". My question to you is: Are you using your light? Are you doing what you were made to do?

Many followers of Jesus are lit (lol). The problem for many of us is not that we aren't using our light, it's that we are only using it in already lit rooms. We have become comfortable in the routines of Christianity. We go to church, we go to bible study, we hang out with our christian friends, and the entire time, our light is shining to people who already have the same light.

These things are great, but we were made for more. We were made to go "public" with what Jesus has done for us. The church is a safe place for the most part. There's not a whole lot of darkness going on (for the most part). It's very comfortable. But a comfortable faith is a lack of faith. Jesus is calling you to uncomfortable places, to dark places - to literally be the light.

We can't have a dangerous theology, but live with comfortable faith.

We are called to go into the night!

I'm a huge College Football fan. The Fall is absolutely my favorite time of the year solely because the Georgia Bulldogs are on my TV every Saturday afternoon. There is nothing like it.
Not everyone has the blessing of rooting for God's favorite football team, however. A few years ago I was in Knoxville, Tennessee to watch my Georgia Bulldogs take on the Tennessee Volunteers. Before the game I was eating at a burger restaurant near the stadium when I met a guy named "Bubba".

True story. That was his real name and he was awesome.

Bubba was decked out from head to toe in Tennessee-orange colors. He had a handlebar mustache that might have been longer than the handlebars on my bicycle. His accent was so southern you could probably order it with a side of mashed potatoes. Bubba's shoes were orange. Bubba's truck was orange. I wouldn't have been surprised if Bubba's wife was orange.

I started talking to Bubba as I was eating my burger, and he told me all about his Saturday Fall routine. He said he would always wake up early and go to *Waffle House* with some of his friends and talk about the Vol's game. Then he'd spend a few hours downtown hanging out with some of his fellow Vols' fans. After that he'd get lunch and listen to other people talk about the Vols on the radio. Then he'd go to the game and sing about the Vols (you know, the Rocky Top Song) all night long.

I admired his passion. After all, at the time I was having this conversation with Bubba, the Tennessee Volunteers hadn't won an SEC Championship in over a decade. They also ended up getting whooped by my Georgia Bulldogs later that day, but that has nothing to do with the story.

Meeting Bubba really made me think. This guy was *all in* for a team that wasn't even going to win. He was so passionate and cared so much about a team that was going to get whooped.
How can people be so passionate about a team that's going to lose, and Jesus followers be dead silent about a team that's already won?

We have something to talk about! We have something to sing about! We have something we should be shouting from the rooftops because Jesus already won the greatest battle of all time when he squared off with death and came out victorious.

1 Corinthians 15:57 says, "But thanks be unto God for He gives us the VICTORY through our Lord JESUS CHRIST."

Jesus has won, Jesus is winning, and Jesus will win again and again.

I'm not going to be quiet about the victory, because the victory can be found in simply trusting in Jesus. Shouldn't we want everyone we come across to join a team that's going to win?

I want to love radically. I want to love loudly. I want to love people who have known nothing but darkness, because that's how good the grace of God is. I can't expect to look like Jesus if I am not willing to go where Jesus went.

Jesus did not go viral with his mission by staying in the light. He loved people in the dark, the hard places where love was absent. Loving people who look like you? That's easy. Loving people who disagree with you? That's like Jesus.

Jesus did not change the world by only loving people who look like him. He changed the world by going after people who looked completely different than Him. Now, we're called to change the world the same way, with Jesus guiding us. We're called to go into the night because it's in the darkness that our light finds the corners of the earth. It's in the night that we truly go viral.
This idea of going viral by going to the hard, dark, and broken places is one that kind of sounds heroic. After all, we are trying to save people's eternities! But it's not without its costs. When you start to love like Jesus, you will also be misunderstood like Jesus. Don't forget that Jesus was so misunderstood and loved so radically that the people of His day killed Him for it.

If people aren't questioning who we are loving and why we are choosing to love them, then we might need to question who we are following.

People talked when Jesus had dinner with the tax collectors. People talked when Jesus took His lunch break with a woman at a well in Samaria. People talked when He let the woman with the bad reputation wash His feet with Her hair. People were always talking about the scandalous ways Jesus's light was shining in the dark!

When people have a hard time understanding how you can give grace to someone, you might be following Jesus. When others don't quite get why you choose to spend time with people with such horrible reputations, you might be following Jesus. When you care so deeply about broken people that you are willing to risk your reputation with your peers so that those people can see the light inside of you, you might be following Jesus.

The light inside of you is stronger than the words of other people.

One night a few years ago, I was headed home after what I thought was an incredible night of ministry. Our young adult gathering was exploding. We had just had close to 500 young people crowded in a building to hear the Gospel and several dozen had responded that night to the word I shared. Those have always been my favorite kind of nights.

I remember pulling into my driveway and looking down at my phone to see I had a voice message from one of our key leaders. I pressed play on the message and this is what I heard:

"Hey Noah, I'm sorry for the late call. I've just had some stuff on my mind. I don't think I'm going to be able to be a part of this ministry anymore. It's starting to make me feel uncomfortable a little bit, if I'm being honest. Tonight I saw several students in the crowd that I know for a fact are not the kind of people we want at our ministry. In fact, the reputation of these students is bringing down the entire reputation of our ministry. I know we are called to win lost people, but it's clear that these people are not being won over based on how they lived the rest of the week. My heart has just been battling this for sometime now and I'm really sorry but I don't think I can handle it any longer. I love you bro and we can talk more later. Bye."

This voice message shook me to my core. This was one of my guys. I trusted this guy with just about everything in our ministry. He was a phenomenal leader, but more than that, he had been a loyal team member since the beginning. This stung.

I remember being so burdened that night as I was sitting in my little car outside of my little apartment. I won't lie: there were some tears. I'm a people pleaser, what can I say? I sat there for some time when I felt God speak something to my spirit. It was not what I thought He was going to say: "Now we are talking."
What?

"Now we are talking. For too long this ministry has been impressive to Christians but looked nothing like me. Loving people with bad reputations looks like me. Now we are talking."

I ended up sitting in my car for over an hour that night praying and worshipping God. It was one of the most powerful encounters with God I've ever had. When it had ended, He gave me the courage to pick back up the phone and call my friend.

I told my friend I understood where he was coming from, but that I wanted him to give it one more week as a part of our ministry.

"I want you to come back and talk to the person you sat next to tonight during service. That guy had never gone to church in his life before a few months ago. Now he doesn't miss a week. I want you to talk to the guy who holds the door for people when they walk in. 9 months ago he was addicted to pornography and felt like he'd never beat it. He hasn't looked at it since. I want you to talk to the girl who comes down to the front during worship. The one who everyone looks at kind of funny. That girl handed me a bottle of pills before service 3 weeks ago. Before service she couldn't let go of the pills but now she can't let go of Jesus! I want you to come back because I think if you'll take another look you'll see that what's actually happening right in front of our eyes is light overcoming dark over and over and over again."

That friend of mine came back like I asked him to. One year after the conversation we hosted an event that saw 1,400 college students and over 200 made decisions for Jesus Christ. Oh yeah, and that friend? He got up on stage that night and shared a part of his testimony. God is really cool like that.

We have to ask God to blow up the comfortable boxes we've put our lives inside. He wants to give grace to people we don't think deserve it. He wants to use people we would never dream of using. He wants us to go into the night after people no one else is willing to chase after!

Are we?

I am not interested in crowding a church building if we are not also crowding Heaven. It's time for the body of Christ to wake up. It's time for us to usher in revival in our cities and our families.

You don't need a microphone or a stage. You don't need to be a pastor or a teacher. You don't even need a title. You don't need anything that you don't already have. How? Because you already have all you need. You have Jesus. You are the LIGHT. It's time to make it go viral.

My junior year of high school I had a best friend. His name was Spencer. Spencer was a stud. Like a STUD, stud. He was extremely athletic, he made great grades and all the girls loved him. We used to walk into the cafeteria together and I would feel really good about myself because of all the girls looking in our direction. Who was I kidding, they were looking in Spencer's direction.

Spencer did have his dark areas of life. He wasn't a follower of Jesus and that showed up from time to time. He would throw massive parties at his house on the weekends. Alcohol was a huge issue for him and he had experienced his fair share of drug use as well. At school, Spencer kind of had a reputation of hanging with a very select group of people. If you didn't fit that "vibe" you probably weren't going to be his friend.
One Tuesday afternoon after football practice I got a phone call from my Mom. She told me Spencer had been in a horrible car wreck and was in the hospital. He had sustained head injuries and they weren't sure if he was going to make it.

I rushed to the hospital.

It felt surreal. Like a bad, bad dream. How could something like this happen?

I remember the family telling us that the doctors thought that even if he did make it, he'd have permanent brain damage. It could potentially cause him to lose speaking capabilities, motor skills - basic life functioning abilities.

But God.

Just a few months later, Spencer returned to school completely healed. All he had to show for his accident was a nasty scar on his scalp. It was truly a miracle. Even the doctors couldn't explain it. The night before Spencer came back to school my Mom told me I needed to invite him to our youth group that night. I said no way. Not a chance I was going to invite this dude to our little youth group. This was the most popular dude in school, I couldn't risk looking like a fool!
I quickly changed my mind when my Mom made it clear that if I wanted dinner that night I better invite Spencer. So that's what I did. And to my surprise, Spencer said yes immediately.

That night at church my youth Pastor gave a message on the grace of God. He talked about what Jesus did for us on the cross by dying for our sins. At the end of his message, he gave an altar call and asked for anyone who wanted to accept Jesus as their Lord and Savior to come down to the front.
Before my youth pastor had even finished talking my friend Spencer took off at a run from our seats on the back row to the front of the room. He laid on the floor weeping. Just a few minutes later he asked Jesus into his heart.

Everything changed that night.

I watched as the next several weeks Jesus changed everything about Spencer. He went from being the guy that only talked to select people to the guy who talked to EVERYBODY. He would literally change lunch tables every single day so that he could try and meet more people. He had more joy than anyone in our school. He gave up the alcohol and the parties and traded them in for a Bible and a notebook that he carried everywhere with him.

He started bringing people to our youth group every single Wednesday night. Our group went from just over 100 students to almost 400 students in a matter of months! Spencer carried so much influence with the other students at our school that when his life changed for Jesus - it literally impacted everyone.

One day I was sitting with Spencer at lunch and I asked him:

"Dude. What happened? Ever since your accident you are a changed man."
Spencer teared up. He sat his fork down on his lunch tray and said:

"I came so close to dying...so now I'm going to live."

I'm not crying, you're crying. Ok I'm crying. At that point I started crying. But then he said words that changed my life forever. They are words that I have written on the inside of every Bible I own:

"You know...the devil should have taken me out when he had the chance. Because now...I'm going to make him pay."

The devil made a huge mistake when he didn't take you out, too. Are you going to make him pay? Are you going to make him pay for not taking you out with the addiction? Are you going to make him pay for not taking you out with the messy family divorce? Are you going to make him regret not killing you with the depression and suicidal thoughts of your past? Are you going to make him pay for all the things in your past that didn't kill you?

It's time to LIVE.

It's time to take the hope you've found in Jesus and take it into the night.

You were made for this. You were made to take this light and to let it reflect from your life into the lives of every single person you encounter. Let the love of Jesus multiply in your life. Let Jesus go viral in every conversation, every random encounter and every relationship in your life.

You want to know how you go viral?

You let what Jesus has done - affect what you are doing today - so that it will change people's eternities tomorrow. As that same process happens in those people's lives, the Gospel will reach even more people.

When you get to heaven you might think you were the cause of 100 people coming to know Jesus. Or 1,000 people. But you'll look up and realize that those 100 reached 1,000 more. Those 1,000 reached 100,000. Those 100,000 reached 1,000,000.
Jesus was the plan. Jesus was the post. Jesus was shared. Jesus went viral.

There's only one thing that will lead to Heaven being crowded.

There's only one thing that will lead to Heaven coming to earth.
There's only one thing that will lead to lives being changed forever.
There's only one thing that will lead to darkness and death being
defeated.

Viral. Jesus.

what now?

1.) Head over to NoahHerrin.org for more resources, including the "Going Viral" Masterclass. This class takes the ideas discussed in this book and goes even deeper. It's a must get.

2.) Share. If this book encouraged or helped you in any way, help make its message viral by sharing it with someone who may need to read it!

Hey!

Thanks for reading my book! Here's a little bit more about me:

I live in Atlanta, GA with my incredible wife Maddy. We travel and talk about Jesus all over the country. It's wild. And amazing. And gives us so much purpose. We also have a really cool community of people here in Atlanta who we chase Jesus with.

I'm currently obsessed with playing golf (my first evolution into dad mode). My golf game needs a lot of prayer though. Speaking of prayer, we think we might want to have kids soon and I don't do messes very well. So pray for Maddy because she'll have to change all the diapers (LOL, she's gonna love this part of the book).

I'm beyond humbled you'd read my book. For real. Thank you. I'd also love to connect with you more. Hit me up on social media @NoahHerrin and let's be friends on this journey together.